DRUGS, ALCOHOL AND MENTAL H...

Alan ...
Formerly ... ...
Bulmer ... College of Higher Education
Reading

Vicky Cornwell
Formerly Principal Social Worker
Basingstoke District Hospital (Psychiatric Division)

CAMBRIDGE
UNIVERSITY PRESS

PUBLISHED BY THE PRESS SYNDICATE OF THE UNIVERSITY OF CAMBRIDGE
The Pitt Building, Trumpington Street, Cambridge, United Kingdom

CAMBRIDGE UNIVERSITY PRESS
The Edinburgh Building, Cambridge CB2 2RU, UK   http://www.cup.cam.ac.uk
40 West 20th Street, New York, NY 10011–4211, USA   http://www.cup.org
10 Stamford Road, Oakleigh, Melbourne 3166, Australia
Ruiz de Alarcón 13, 28014 Madrid, Spain

First published 1987
Reprinted 1988
Second edition 1993
Reprinted 1994, 1997, 2000

Printed in the United Kingdom at the University Press, Cambridge

Typeface Palatino   *System* Monotype Lasercomp   [VN]

A catalogue record for this book is available from the British Library

ISBN 0 521 43710 5 paperback

Cover photo: Young man in narcotic sleep (Oscar Burriel/Latin Stock/Science
Photo Library)

The publisher would like to thank the following for permission to reproduce
illustrations: cover photograph Science Photo Library; fig 4.2 Royal Botanic
Gardens, Kew; fig 5.1 from Clapham, Tutin & Warburg *Flora of the British Isles,
Illustrations,* CUP; figs 7.1, 8.1 & 8.2 Health Education Authority; fig 7.2 UNESCO;
fig 7.3 Transport Research Laboratory; fig 12.3 from Gibbons *Psychiatry,*
Butterworth-Heinemann.

Contents

Preface

Preface

This book is primarily concerned with biochemical, behavioural and social influences which affect the function of the mind. The majority of human societies incorporate the use of drugs, legally or illegally, which influence mental activity. These may be used to alter and enhance aspects of mental function or to diminish activity and so reduce tensions or the appreciation of problems. Chapters are included that deal with all the major groups of drugs which are misused, that is hypnotics, tranquilisers, stimulants, euphoriants such as alcohol and organic solvents, hallucinogens and narcotics. Many of these drugs, by virtue of interfering with the biochemistry of the brain, mimic or induce behaviours which are considered to be outside the limits of mental health.

Although not getting the major publicity, alcohol is the main problem drug in most developed countries and, because of Western influence, also in many less-developed societies. The biological basis of the effects of alcohol on the human body is described and the medical and social problems arising from alcohol misuse are discussed. The chapters following this consider the control of alcohol consumption and the help which is available for problem drinkers.

The final chapters are concerned with the main forms of mental illness prevalent in Western society and a survey of the changing pattern of care for the mentally ill in the United Kingdom.

The authors wish to acknowledge the help received from many people, in particular Dr David Battin, Consultant Psychogeriatrician at Newtown Hospital, Worcester, Mr Graham Fanti, Director of the Hereford and Worcester Alcohol Advisory Service, Mr Ray Johnson, librarian at Alcohol Concern, Mr Dennis Clare, Deputy Clerk to the Justices in Worcestershire and Detective Chief Inspector Jones and his colleagues in the West Mercia Police Drug Squad. We would also like to thank Mr David Sykes for reading and commenting on the manuscript.

Drugs and drug abuse

1.1 Definition of a drug

The first major problem in considering drug abuse is to define a drug. This is difficult because in general conversation the word is used in many different ways. Many people for example do not think of alcohol, aspirin or nicotine as being drugs. Others use 'drug' when they really mean narcotics whilst another group would include any manufactured chemical in the list.

The following are some examples of definitions which have been used in a more specific context.

'Any substance used in the composition of a medicine.'

This includes many of the commonly used substances, but it excludes some commonly used ones such as nicotine and tetrahydrocannabinol in cannabis.

'Any chemical substance which alters a mood, perception or consciousness and is used to the apparent detriment of society.'

This includes most of the substances which are misused by people but excludes many medically useful substances such as sulphonamides or even aspirin.

'Any substance taken into the body which brings about a physiological change.'

This definition also creates problems as it includes substances such as basic nutrients and water but possibly excludes some psychotropic drugs, though in time all of these may prove to bring about their effects by some physiological change.

'Any substance which when taken into the body may modify one or more of its physical or mental functions.'

This is probably the best working definition to use as it does not exclude any substances which are considered to be drugs but it does perhaps include some, like water or nutrients, which are not usually thought of as being drugs.

1.2 Legal and illegal drug use

Many drugs come into the category of being socially acceptable and legally used and it is an interesting exercise to list the drugs one uses. The list is not quite A–Z but does stretch from antiperspirants to wind relievers. There are of course some drug-containing substances, such as cannabis, which are socially acceptable to some sections of the population and these are considered later along with other substances whose self-prescribed use is illegal in our society. Society's acceptance of drugs does change and the use of tobacco is now much less acceptable than it was 20 years ago. It may be that other drugs will become legal and socially acceptable at some future time. It is unlikely, however, that any of the presently accepted drugs will cease to be used entirely. Attempts to outlaw alcohol in the USA or India and opium in the Far East all failed and there are no examples of drugs, once built into the fabric of a society, being completely eliminated. At present the most used drugs in this category are caffeine, nicotine, ethanol (alcohol) and minor pain-killers such as aspirin and paracetamol.

By far the largest group of drugs contains those which are used medically to control illness by producing physical or mental changes within the body. The vast majority of these are not, nor are they likely to be, used illegally by individuals to produce desired changes in body function. Some are obtained by and are misused by a few people but this misuse does not constitute a major medical or social problem.

There are however many drugs which are self-administered but whose use in this way is not legal and is not acceptable to the majority of society. These drugs are all **psychotropic** drugs, that is, they have an effect on the activity of the **psyche** or mind. Some of them may be legally available for use under medical supervision, for example barbiturates, amphetamines or morphine. Others, such as organic solvents, are available for use other than as drugs but if taken into the body have psychotropic effects. Then there is a final group, the various hallucinogens, whose only use is for producing non-medical psychotropic effects.

1.3 Types of drug abuse

There are many reasons why some people become involved in drug abuse, though often this is only a transient phase. Many young people try one or more of the available drugs out of curiosity or because of peer group pressures but do not become regular users. Some do remain occasional users, however, and others, often quite quickly, become dependent on their drug dose. It is possible therefore to categorise drug abusers, but it must be remembered that some people change their behaviour and move from one category to another.

Experimenters

These are people who try a drug once or maybe a few times but then cease to use it. The cessation is usually due to a bad experience, a common phenomenon for a novice drug abuser. Sometimes, though, it may be due to a fear of the harmful effects of the drug or of becoming dependent upon it. Tobacco, marijuana and amphetamines are the main examples of drugs which many people experiment with but do not continue to use.

Take it or leave it

With many of the so-called 'soft drugs' there are large numbers of people who indulge fairly regularly but at intervals. These people have no compulsion to continue usage but do so when they are in conducive places or in the company of other users. Most marijuana and amphetamine abusers come into this category as do the large majority of alcohol drinkers. There are some people who only occasionally smoke tobacco but the large majority of tobacco users are under some compulsion to continue. When one considers the 'hard drugs' very few people who become involved are able to stay with occasional use. A small number of people are known to be able to take heroin once a week without increasing the dose and they remain able to function normally within society. These are however the few exceptions and with a drug as dependence-forming as heroin the only safe assumption is that if the drug is used at all, dependence and its disastrous consequences will follow.

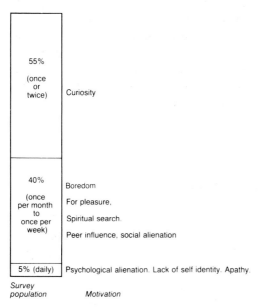

Figure 1.1 The motivation for drug consumption (nicotine and alcohol not included) in 16–25-year-old American survey respondents with an indication of the frequency of use and the percentage of respondents involved.

Compulsive users

This is the smallest category for most drugs including alcohol (even though compared with other drugs except tobacco, the number of compulsive users is large). This group consists of those who must use the drug at regular intervals, usually several times a day, and whose drug abuse often interferes with normal social and economic functioning. In these people there is at least a craving for the drug but often a physical and/or psychological dependence on the drug with unpleasant symptoms if the drug is unavailable for any reason. There are specific terms used for these people in the drug sub-culture, for example **pot-heads** for compulsive marijuana users, **speed freaks** for amphetamine users and **junkies** for those dependent upon narcotics. Although the majority of compulsive alcohol users are not members of a drug sub-culture they are subsumed under the term **alcoholics**. Note that some alcoholics do, either voluntarily or because of circumstances, opt out of society.

Why some people progress to this stage and others do not is unknown. Where illegal drugs are concerned, compulsive users are often socially and sexually immature and are having problems adjusting in society. Such personality inadequacy is typical of many people involved in other forms of deviant behaviour as well as with drug problems, and environmental factors such as peer group pressure and access to particular drugs are also important. Unfortunately drug access is becoming progressively easier as illegal drug trafficking increases.

Apart from access there is also the influence of physiological, social and psychological factors affecting an individual's response to the drug. The drug itself produces varied levels of response in different people taking the same dose, and of course in each person effects vary with change in dosage used. Body mass, the sex of the individual and the presence of other drugs will also change the physiological effects produced. The social setting, the personality and the mood of the user at the time of use are also important. For example, alcohol may calm a person who is stressed but will stimulate the same person if he or she happens to be among friends at a party. The psychological effects are often altered by the expectation of a user. If a 'high' is anticipated then the chances are that it will occur and similarly the expectation of an unpleasant experience (bad trip) is very likely to produce one.

1.4 Centrally acting drugs

Most of the drugs of misuse have effects on the central nervous system (CNS) with or without peripheral effects. Fifty years ago, Lewin produced a now-classic categorisation of drugs based on their behavioural, social and experienced effects. Although it is usual now to use a different classification and some groups of drugs such as tranquilisers were not known at the time,

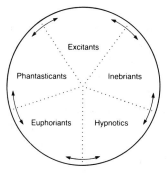

Figure 1.2 Lewin's classification of drugs acting on the central nervous system.

Lewin's schema is a useful starting point for considering drugs and makes an interesting comparison with the modern sub-division. Lewin divided the centrally acting drugs into five groups and placed them in a circle (figure 1.2) thus emphasising the fact that many drugs have multiple effects. His groups of drugs were as follows:

Excitants are substances which cause central nervous system stimulation. Caffeine and amphetamines fall into this group. All these drugs bring about behavioural arousal.

Inebriants cause intoxication. Initially they bring about behavioural excitement but this is soon followed by depression. Alcohol and many organic solvents are examples of inebriants.

Hypnotics are the sleep-inducing agents including both anaesthetics and sedatives.

Euphoriants act by blotting out perception of the real world and replacing it with one in which the individual perceives no problems. The opiates are the main euphoriants.

Phantasticants are drugs which substitute an alternative but equally real world for the present one. The new world is characterised by abnormal sensory perception and there is memory of the drug-induced world after the effect of the drug has worn off. LSD and its allies belong to this group.

Of Lewin's terms, only hypnotics is in general use now. His excitants are now usually called stimulants, euphoriants are known as narcotics and phantasticants are hallucinogens. The general grouping of inebriants no longer really exists as the various drugs producing intoxication tend to be referred to separately.

1.5 Patterns of drug abuse

Although the terms **soft** and **hard** drugs tend not to be used now, the majority of users start with the so-called soft drugs such as marijuana or amphetamines, but a more important point is that most soft drug users have previously had experience of one or both of the legal drugs, nicotine and alcohol.

When people start using soft drugs, this is usually in addition to nicotine and alcohol, even in the case of young teenagers. The same principle applies to those who graduate on to hard drugs. There are very few drug abusers who use only one drug. Some constantly use drug cocktails where often one drug counteracts unwanted effects of another, whilst others are generalised users who take whichever drug happens to be available. There is also a process of progression of use from soft to hard drugs, though it must be remembered that most users of soft drugs do not progress to hard and a small minority of hard drug users have not previously used soft ones.

1.6 Size of the illegal drug problem

The statistics of drug misusers only register those who have come to the notice of the authorities and so only represent a small proportion of the drug-misusing population. Over the past few years the number of new addicts notified to the Home Office has remained fairly constant at around 6000. However the total number of addicts during each year has shown a steady rise of about 2000 per year. The great majority of registered addicts are addicted to heroin with addiction to methadone or cocaine being the next most important, although each of these groups is small in comparison. In 1989 there were 4883 new heroin addicts registered in the United Kingdom whilst new addicts to methadone numbered 682 and new addicts to cocaine numbered 527. Over two-thirds of the addicts are male and over half are in the age group 21–9 years. Less than 10% are under the age of 21. Surveys of school children show that under the age of 16, less than 1% ever use drugs other than solvents or cannabis.

The total number of people convicted of drug offences is continuing to rise having reached over 30 500 in 1988. Cannabis dominates police drug enforcement activities with over 26 000 convictions or cautions in 1988. Amphetamines with over 2500 and heroin with over 1800 were the next most common.

Seizures of drugs vary in amount from year to year but the general trend is upwards. The majority of seizures are of cannabis resin, there being nearly 22 000 in 1988. Cannabis apart, amphetamines, cocaine and heroin are the most important drugs at present. In 1991 the seizures of all of these drugs were double those in 1990. The police assume that this is a measure of the level of illegal import of drugs rather than a significant increase in the percentage of attempted imports seized. In particular, the rise in seizures of amphetamines and cocaine mark the arrival of ecstasy and crack respectively on the British drug scene.

1.7 Some relevant terms

Abstinence syndrome

This is the particular group of physical and psychological symptoms which occurs when the drug is withheld from the drug-dependent person. The nature of the abstinence syndrome varies with the drug on which dependence exists. It may also be known as withdrawal syndrome. For most drugs the symptoms disappear after a time when the body has recovered its normal state. Medical help may be needed to overcome the symptoms and a residual desire to take the drug again may last almost indefinitely. Willpower is needed to resist the temptation to use the drug again.

Addiction

This term is still widely used but gradually its use is being replaced by the term drug dependence (see below).

Drug abuse

This is the occasional or persistent excessive use of a drug for personal gratification. It should not be confused with **misuse** which implies medical or lay use of a drug to treat a disease, not considered appropriate by the majority of medical opinion.

Drug dependence

A person is drug dependent if he or she feels compelled to take the drug on a periodic or continuous basis in order to experience its psychic effect or to avoid the discomfort produced by its absence. For descriptive purposes it can be divided into two types.

Physical dependence is when the drug or one of its metabolites has become necessary for the continued functioning of the body. This means that on withdrawal of the drug there are definitely physical symptoms, often very unpleasant for the dependent person – the abstinence syndrome is caused. It should be noted that in addition to the overt physical symptoms, psychological ones also occur which are a manifestation of the withdrawal effects on the brain.

Psychological dependence consists of just emotional components with no physical symptoms on withdrawal. The emotional changes which occur when the drug is withheld may amount to only mild discomfiture or may be such that the person is led to persist in using the drug. At its extreme, psychological dependence may lead to changes in lifestyle and behaviour where life revolves round drug taking and the company of others likewise involved. In these circumstances the individual may live in a sub-culture of drug users separated by law or behaviour from normal society.

Habituation

A mild form of dependence where withdrawal does not result in severe abstinence symptoms but which is noticed by the person and may cause slight, short-term discomfort or craving for the drug.

Tolerance

This is the need to use increasing doses of the drug to produce the same effect. It may depend on changed sensitivity of cell receptors, on increased rates of metabolism of the drug or on changes in cell transmitter substances.

Socially acceptable drugs

2.1 Introduction

Thousands of substances which come within the definition of 'drugs' are in use every day and many of them in enormous quantities. For the purposes of this book, drugs which are used under medical supervision will be ignored, but this still leaves a large number. Most of these have little noticeable effect on the nervous system and are unlikely to cause any severe physical effects unless used vastly to excess. For example, antiperspirants can, if used too much, cause skin problems, and throat lozenges or cough medicines should not be used more frequently than indicated by the instructions on the container. The most important self-administered drugs and by far the most frequently used are caffeine, minor pain-killers (aspirin and paracetamol), nicotine and alcohol.

2.2 Caffeine

This drug is found in four of the most commonly used drinks in our society, that is tea, coffee, cola and cocoa. Tea and cocoa also contain other drugs with similar effects. These are **theophylline** in tea and **theobromine** in cocoa.

Caffeine is a stimulant drug. It acts in the brain by reducing the breakdown of **cyclic AMP** and so acts on the **catecholamine** pathways. Catecholamines (adrenalin and noradrenalin) control stimulatory pathways and act by increasing the levels of cyclic AMP in the brain cells. The noticeable effects of caffeine are to remove feelings of tiredness, increase the ability to think clearly, stimulate the heart muscle, relax the muscles of the bronchioles and also act as a diuretic. When used medically as a stimulant the usual dose is 100–300 mg. A dose of 1000 mg produces sleep difficulties, restlessness, trembling and possibly seeing flashes of light. Table 2.1 gives the dosages of caffeine obtained from standard measures of common drinks.

Although it is often stated that caffeine only produces habituation it does, in fact, produce a physical dependence. One of the major effects of caffeine is to increase wakefulness. However, a commonly ascribed attribute, that of removing the effects of excess alcohol intake, is fallacious. If one takes

Table 2.1 Dosages of caffeine in standard measures of drinks

Drink	Caffeine dose (mg)
cocoa	50–200
cola	35–55
coffee	100–200
tea	50–100

strong black coffee when drunk one simply becomes wide awake and drunk rather than being sleepy and drunk. Thus it is safer not to drink the coffee but to sleep off the effects of the alcohol.

2.3 Minor pain-killers

Aspirin (acetyl salicylic acid)

This is a very useful drug as it is not only a minor pain-killer (analgesic) but is also a good anti-inflammatory agent and an anti-pyretic (reduces temperature). It is found in natural products, for example in willow bark which was used as an analgesic in the eighteenth century.

Although there have been attempts to reduce the self-administration of aspirin, there are still upwards of 2000 million tablets sold each year in Britain. They are mainly used to relieve headache, toothache and pains in muscles and joints. Aspirin is a good analgesic for minor to moderate pains. If two aspirin do not bring relief it is unlikely that further administration will bring any effect.

Insoluble aspirin is not now recommended for use as in about 70% of the population it causes some bleeding from the stomach lining. However this is usually too slight to be detected other than by special tests for occult blood in faeces or by gastroscopy. It is especially likely to cause stomach bleeding if taken after alcohol. Soluble aspirin which is buffered by being in an alkaline solution does not cause this problem. A few people are allergic to aspirin and will develop symptoms such as nettle rash or asthmatic attacks on administration of the drug.

It is thought that aspirin produces its effects in the brain by inhibiting synthesis of **prostaglandins** which are mediators of inflammation and possibly both pain and pyrexia. Aspirin also seems to prevent the production of prostaglandins at sites of injury having penetrated the cell membranes by an insulin-dependent process.

Paracetamol

This is a mild pain-killer and anti-pyretic but does not have any anti-inflammatory properties. It does not cause any stomach damage but may damage the liver or kidneys if taken in large overdose such as 40–50 tablets. It has replaced **phenacetin** which is a good pain-killer but which is much more likely to cause kidney damage. In the body, phenacetin is converted to paracetamol and so it is much more sensible to use the less harmful product. Its mode of action is not known for certain but like aspirin it may work by preventing prostaglandin production though only in a limited number of cell types.

2.4 Nicotine

Nicotine is the drug component of tobacco smoke. If one smokes cigarettes and inhales the smoke, a dose of about 3 mg of nicotine per cigarette is received. The fatal dose is 40 mg and so a packet of 20 contains more than a fatal dose. However, even a chain smoker could not take a fatal dose this way as not all the nicotine is absorbed and the blood level would never reach the fatal level.

Although many adult smokers have given up smoking, 1990 figures suggest that 20% of men and 10% of women still remain in the heavy smoker category, that is smoking more than 20 cigarettes per day. More disturbing are the figures that 5% of 13 year olds and 20% of 15 year olds smoke at least one cigarette per day. 30% of older teenagers are regular smokers, averaging 11–12 cigarettes per day.

Nicotine acts on the **cholinergic** pathways in the brain, behaving first as a stimulant and then as a depressant, but in ordinary smoking the effects are largely reflex from the stimulation of chemoreceptors in the aortic and carotid bodies, the pulmonary circulation and the left ventricle.

When smoking one cigarette, on average 1 mg of nicotine is absorbed. This stimulates the sympathetic system causing vasoconstriction in the skin, vasodilation in the muscles, increase in the rate of heart beat and rise in the blood pressure. In a novice smoker a major effect is to stimulate the vomit centre but this effect disappears after a short time. The effects of nicotine (or of smoking in general) seem to be largely psychological. Some smokers report sedative effects whilst others report stimulation. The effect also seems to vary with the circumstances in which smoking takes place, with the dose of nicotine received and also with the person's mood at the time. There is also much difference of opinion as to whether smokers are habituated to or are dependent upon nicotine and, if there is dependence, whether it is physical or psychological. Apart from the nicotine, there are many other components in tobacco smoke and most of them have harmful effects. These are discussed in *Human Physical Health* by Dennis Taylor, another book in this series.

2.5 Alcohol

There are many different alcohols but, in the context of drug use, alcohol is a synonym for **ethyl alcohol** (ethanol). This is produced by the fermentation of sugars by micro-organisms, in particular by yeasts. It has been an important **psychotropic** (mind altering) drug for thousands of years. There are references to production of alcoholic drinks in many of the ancient manuscripts, for example Noah planted a vineyard and it is probable that alcohol has been in use since Neolithic times when people started to store plant material for food. Almost any plant material can be fermented to produce ethanol, but the most used materials are grapes and cereal grains, with the sap of palm trees also being used in many tropical countries.

Alcohol has many effects on the body and also is a major cause of social problems. In Western society it is probably the most important drug of abuse and will be dealt with in some detail in chapters 6–9.

Misuse of prescribed and related drugs

3.1 Introduction

There are many drugs prescribed which are addictive and are also used for non-medical purposes. There are two aspects to the problem of these drugs – the middle-aged and elderly who have become dependent as a result of over-prescription, and the young who obtain them illegally and use them as mood changing agents. Three main groups of drugs need to be considered, **hypnotics** (sleep-inducing agents), **sedatives** (minor tranquilisers) and **stimulants**.

3.2 Hypnotics and minor tranquilisers

By definition, hypnotics are sleep inducers whilst sedatives are used to quieten or reduce anxiety without inducing sleep. In a sense, the sub-division is artificial as the difference in action is often due to the dose level or the setting in which the drug is used.

Barbiturates

The chemical **barbituric acid** was first synthesised in 1864 by von Baeyer and, although not itself a depressant of the central nervous system, it is the parent of a large number of drugs which have depressant properties. Of the 2500 derivatives which have been prepared, about 50 have been used clinically. The main way in which they vary is in the length of time over which they are active. Some examples are given in table 3.1.

Phenobarbitone is little used now except sometimes as an anti-convulsive to control epilepsy.

Pentothal is used as a premedication for surgery and also as an intravenous dental anaesthetic.

The main problems are from the medium-term barbiturates. These have been widely used as sleeping tablets and they are the ones favoured by illegal users. They are favoured for street use as both the onset and duration times are right and the drugs produce little hang-over effect.

Table 3.1 Examples of available barbiturates

Period of action	Time for onset	Chemical name	Common name
long – up to 24 hours	gradual	phenobarbitone	—
medium – 3–12 hours	15–30 minutes	pentobarbitone	nembutal
		quinalbarbitone	seconal
		amylobarbitone	amytal
		butobarbitone	soneryl
		quinalbarbitone + amylobarbitone	tuinal
short – up to 15 minutes	immediate	thiopentane	pentothal

The general effect of barbiturates on the central nervous system is to depress activity. In low doses, barbiturates depress post-synaptic sensitivity to transmitters, whilst in higher doses they prevent transmitter release from the pre-synaptic membranes. Both these effects may be due to a reduction in membrane permeability to sodium ions and potassium ions. Many brain pathways are affected but particularly those whose transmitters are acetylcholine, serotonin, noradrenalin or glutamate. There seem to be specific barbiturate binding sites on neurone membranes. The activity of these appears to enhance the inhibitory effect of **gamma aminobutyric acid (GABA)** which is a major inhibitory neurotransmitter.

The degree of effect varies with the type of drug used, the dose level and both the physiological and psychological state of the user. A barbiturate taken when a person wishes to go to sleep has an effect different from that taken primarily for its intoxication effect at a social gathering. At low doses the drug seems to affect the cortical areas of the brain and the effects spread to the sub-cortical areas when the dose is increased. Another major effect of barbiturates is to depress the activity of the respiratory centres in the brain which is why higher doses can be fatal, particularly if combined with alcohol which is also a depressant.

The major medical use of medium-term barbiturates is to produce sleep by depressing the activity of the **reticular activating system** in the brain stem. They are effective in producing sleep but it is not normal in its pattern. In particular there is a reduction in the amount of REM sleep. This form of sleep, in which there is rapid eye movement and during which a person dreams, seems to be necessary and a chronic barbiturate user will catch up on dreaming on withdrawal of the drug. These dreams are often very vivid and disturbing.

Both acute and chronic overdoses of barbiturates produce symptoms resembling those of too much alcohol intake including slowness of speech, difficulty in thinking, poor memory, faulty judgement and an exaggeration of basic personality traits. Changes in behaviour are common but none of them is characteristic just of barbiturate abuse.

At the present time, barbiturates are relatively unimportant on the illegal market. This seems due to the preference by addicts for benzodiazepines rather than barbiturates and also the relatively easy availability of heroin.

Tolerance to barbiturates develops in two ways. Repeated doses activate the liver enzymes which detoxify the drug and so it is removed from the body more quickly, whilst the CNS becomes adapted to its presence and so higher doses are needed to produce an effect. Unlike some other drugs, however, tolerance to barbiturate does not seem to increase the lethal dose.

Both psychological and physical dependence develop. There is a strong desire to continue taking the drug which may be due to a need for the euphoria or a wish to avoid the abstinence symptoms. The physical dependence is because the body physiology responds to an absence of the drug by **rebound hyperactivity**. Systems which have been depressed by the drug's presence become hyperactive and so produce very unpleasant and possibly life-threatening symptoms.

The abstinence syndrome begins to appear within 24 hours of cessation of drug taking, reaches a peak in two to three days and then gradually subsides. At first the user has feelings of anxiety, involuntary twitching of muscles and unintentional tremor of the hands and fingers. As the withdrawal progresses, there is increasing muscular weakness, dizziness and disturbances of visual perception. Later, nausea may develop and there may be convulsions similar to grand-mal epilepsy. If a person withdraws under medical supervision, initially there is treatment of the symptoms and gradually the dose of barbiturate is reduced. This treatment deals with the physical symptoms but some form of psychotherapy may be needed to remove the psychological dependence.

Non-barbiturate hypnotics

These have effects similar to barbiturates but different chemical structures. Some, such as chloral hydrate and paraldehyde have been used as sleep inducers since the last century whilst others are of recent manufacture. Many of these latter such as **Doriden** (glutethimide) and **Mandrax** (methaqualone with diphenhydramines) were originally thought to be non-addictive but are now known to be so and have abstinence symptoms similar to those of barbiturates. All of these substances may be obtained by theft or other illegal means for street use and are used as alternatives to barbiturates.

Minor tranquilisers

There are two major varieties of these — meprobamate, marketed as **Miltown** or **Equanil**, and the benzodiazepines marketed as **Valium**, **Librium** and **Oblivon**. The injectable form of the benzodiazepine **Temazepam** has become a street drug of choice, particularly in Scotland. In 1990 the price for benzodiazepines in tablet or capsule form was £1 for four 5 mg tablets. Supply is entirely from stolen or prescribed tranquilisers, there is no illicit manufacture. Although there has been a steady decline in tranquiliser prescriptions since the late 1970s, the level of prescription is still high, 23 000 000 tablets being prescribed in 1988.

Meprobamate was first synthesised in 1951 and soon replaced phenobarbitone as an anxiety depressant. Its main action in the brain seems to be to raise the threshold for the stimulation of the limbic system and so depress the emotions. It does not seem to have any effects on either the adrenergic or cholinergic pathways. The benzodiazepines also depress electrical discharge in the limbic system and raise the threshold for behavioural arousal. They can also be used as hypnotics causing some depression of REM sleep and markedly reducing stage 4 sleep (the slow wave, deep sleep phase).

All these drugs may produce drowsiness as a side effect and all of them give rise to physical dependence when used over a long period in high doses. The abstinence syndrome produced is very similar to that of barbiturates but may run a more protracted course and there is a relatively greater prominence of perceptual symptoms. Their use in conjunction with other CNS depressants can be very dangerous because of synergistic effects causing fatal depression of the respiratory centres. These are effects where the combined action of the two drugs is greater than the sum of the separate effects.

3.3 Stimulants

These drugs are called stimulants as they increase the activity of mood elevating regions in the brain, that is they stimulate adrenergic nerves and so are also known as **sympathomimetic** compounds. The amphetamines are the most commonly used and abused drugs in this group, but cocaine is the stimulant which has been longest in use and is now becoming a major drug of misuse in Western society.

Amphetamines

The first amphetamine, **benzedrine**, was manufactured in 1927 and since then many others have been produced. When amphetamines were being widely prescribed by doctors, theft was the main source for the illegal market. The illegal use of amphetamine fell during the mid-1980s but there has been a considerable increase in recent years. The main difference is that amphetamine sulphate manufactured illegally has become the most important source. Large quantities are available on the illegal market and amphetamine is at present the second most popular stimulant in the illicit market after cannabis. Amphetamine is often heavily diluted with adulterants down to 10% purity or less. The street price is £10–15 per gram.

Clinically the amphetamines have been used to help weight loss, to treat narcolepsy (inability to stay awake), fatigue and also depressive states. They work by releasing newly synthesised catecholamines in the brain and interfering with their re-uptake and inactivation. Therefore they increase the activity in nerve pathways which use noradrenalin or dopamine as the neurotransmitter. These pathways are involved in stimulating cardiac output and muscular activity as well as mood elevation, hence the clinical use of the drugs. The non-medical user is seeking the same effects and so uses these drugs as 'uppers' to feel alert, wakeful and immune to fatigue. Clinically and non-clinically it is usual to take the drug orally as it is readily absorbed throughout the intestinal mucosa. However a very quick and intense high can be produced if amphetamine is injected intravenously. When used in this way it is known as **speed** or **splash**. An increasing problem is **freebasing**. The amphetamine sulphate is separated into its basic (amphetamine) and acidic (sulphate) components. The 'free base' amphetamine is injected.

Except in highly susceptible people, any toxic effects from amphetamine are due to excessive doses being taken. An overdose results in restlessness, tremor, hyperactive reflexes, irritability, insomnia, anxiety and occasionally hallucinations and delirium. There may also be dangerous increases in blood pressure and cardiac arrhythmias. A person who regularly uses amphetamine and has gradually increased the dosage over several months may develop a drug-induced psychosis which resembles paranoid schizophrenia (see chapter 12). Tolerance to the central stimulating effects develops and the chronic user has to increase the dosage to obtain the mood elevating effects. However tolerance does not develop to all the toxic effects and so the manifestations of toxic use can be very severe. Normal clinical dosages are usually below 15 mg per day, and at this level toxic effects are unusual. In a report on amphetamine abuse in the San Francisco area a characteristic pattern of use was shown amongst addicts where oral doses reached 150–250 mg per day and then were replaced by 20–40 mg intravenous doses three or four times a day. These doses produced marked toxic effects in users but without persuading them to seek help to overcome the dependence on the drug.

Speed users may keep up the injections for several days during which they do not eat or sleep. When the injections are discontinued the individual enters a reaction phase or crash. If fortunate, the user may just fall asleep, totally exhausted, or he may go into amphetamine psychosis. It should be noted that a profound depressive state can occur following withdrawal of amphetamines. Along with the psychotic personality change, there is often a great fascination with the needle, with the injection itself becoming the reward. Another drug-taking pattern which may develop is a form of up/down drug cycle, amphetamine-barbiturate-amphetamine (the other form is heroin-cocaine-heroin).

Speed users are usually under 30 years old as older people cannot withstand the physical strain. Trips last typically 36–72 hours with a crash lasting several days. Such a lifestyle is incompatible with life in normal society and having a steady job is impossible. The result is that speed users form their own sub-culture, but it should be noted that the association is based not on friendship but merely on drug use.

Ecstasy

This is a derivative of amphetamine, **methylenedioxymethamphetamine** (MDMA). This drug is a hallucinogen and stimulant. It has only been available in quantity since 1988, at which time it was strongly associated with Acid House music and parties. Since then it has become widespread and is now readily available all over the country. It is usually sold as white tablets, but is also found as pink, yellow or clear capsules. Street prices range from £10–25 per unit. In the early 1990s ecstasy is considered by the police to be one of the major illegal drug problems.

Cocaine

The leaves of the coca plant (*Erythroxylon coca*) have been used as a stimulant in Peru since about AD 1000 (see figure 3.1). Originally it was used in religious observances amongst the Inca nobility but then its use spread to all classes in that society. The Spaniards introduced it to Europe in the sixteenth century but it never became widely used. The active ingredient, cocaine, was isolated in 1858 when it was used as a local anaesthetic, then as a cure for morphine dependence. This latter was supported by Freud who used it also to treat his own depression. In the late nineteenth century coca was used as an ingredient in patent medicines and in the soft drink Coca-cola. By 1906 its use in Coca-cola had ceased but there is in fact no evidence that the small amounts used in soft drinks would be in any way harmful.

Cocaine has marked stimulating effects on the central and sympathetic nervous systems but does not cause physical dependence. Its effects on the user are very similar to those of amphetamine but with an intense feeling of euphoria. The most common method of administration is as a snuff but continued use in this way can lead to lesions or perforations developing in the nasal septum because of the localised vasoconstriction caused by the drug. Many users progress from sniffing to intravenous injections, the drug being taken alone or in combination with heroin. Those who inject cocaine regard it as the ultimate drug experience with exaggerated feelings of

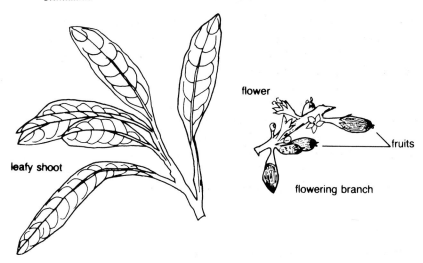

Figure 3.1 The coca plant (*Erythroxylon coca*) from the leaves of which cocaine is extracted.

physical strength and mental capacity. However, cocaine is metabolised very rapidly and repeated large injections are needed at frequent intervals to maintain the 'high'. If this pattern of use is continued, feelings of anxiety and suspicion replace the original euphoria and a condition similar to that of amphetamine psychosis may occur. There is also a danger of acute cocaine poisoning leading to anxiety, confusion, irregular respiration, high pulse rate, sensation of crawling objects on the skin and nausea. Death may occur, due to respiratory arrest or convulsions.

Home Office statistics on the number and size of seizures by both the police and customs suggest a continued and increased spread of cocaine use. Typical prices in 1990 were £80–100 per gram for cocaine which is 50–70% pure. A typical 'weekend' user may consume $\frac{1}{4}$ g over a weekend. A regular user with adequate financial resources might consume 1–2 g per day.

Crack

Crack is the smokable form of cocaine. Cocaine freebase is formed by chemical extraction from cocaine hydrochloride and, as this is volatile, it can be smoked. Cocaine is reacted with some simple household chemicals. The dried product is lumps of cocaine in smokable form, 'cocaine rocks'. These are then cracked into small pieces for sale.

When smoked, a small amount of cocaine crack produces a rapid but short-lived high. The intense high only lasts for a few minutes and then is followed by depression. Dependence on crack develops very rapidly.

A single dose is not very expensive but because of the depression and dependence, users can spend a lot of money on crack.

Crack is becoming very common, particularly in the large English cities. The cost in 1990 was about £20 for 0.2 g. A dependent user can get through several grams at a stretch and so the dependence can become very expensive. The increasing occurrence of freebasing cocaine and its becoming available to all sections of the population is one of the major worries for the Police Drug Squads.

3.4 Other prescription drugs

Any drug which has a stimulant or euphoric effect is liable to be misused, thus many prescribed drugs are misused at one time or another. At the present time there are two prescribed drugs frequently misused.

Temgesic is a strong analgesic which is available in ampoules for injection or in tablet form. It produces some euphoria which is the reason for its misuse. Hallucinations and psychomimetic effects also occur.

Amyl nitrite is used as a stimulant to treat some heart conditions. In the misusers market it is sold as English poppers. They are mainly bought by gay men to enhance sexual activity and to loosen inhibitions in dancing. The inhaled vapour gives a short-lived rush. A similar drug, butyl nitrite, imported from the USA is on sale in sex shops and gay clubs.

3.5 Solvent abuse (glue sniffing)

Many substances are easily available which are not intended to be used as drugs but which have intoxicant properties. In each case the intoxicant is an organic solvent or an aerosol propellant gas. Inhaling intoxicants is not a new problem, the origin probably being the use of nitrous oxide, ether and chloroform in the nineteenth century. This was very much a minority problem until the development of modern glues, solvents and so on over the past 30 years. The main problem substances and their active agents are shown in table 3.2. Glue sniffing first came to light as a problem amongst children and teenagers in the 1960s, the solvent in the glue being used to achieve an altered state of awareness or a state of intoxication. Glues or other semi-solid substances are placed into plastic bags and the volatile solvent is inhaled from the bag. Liquids are placed on cotton wool in a bag and aerosols are breathed through a rag filter which traps the solid particles. Because of the very large area for absorption in the lungs, intake is very rapid. The substances sniffed usually have a depressant effect on the CNS, but also cause confusion, un-coordination, dizziness often with delusions and both visual and auditory hallucinations. Some of these substances, for example butane and trichloroethane which are in fact two of the most misused substances at present, cause stimulation of the heart. This stimulation is brought about by the increased production of adrenalin. Thus it is clear that

Table 3.2 Products commonly used for sniffing and their active agents

Product	Active agent
Glues	Acetone
	N-hexane
	Toluene
Plastic cement	Acetone
	Toluene
Correcting fluid	Acetone
Correcting fluid thinner	Trichloroethane
Nail polish and remover	Amyl acetate
Dry cleaning fluid	Carbon tetrachloride
Dyes	Acetone
	Methylene chloride
Hair lacquers	Ethanol
	Methanol
Rubber solutions	Benzene
	Chloroform
	Hexane
Aerosols	
Car paints	Isobutane
Damp start	Freon propellants
De-icer	Trichlorofluoromethane
Gas lighter fuel	Dichlorodifluoromethane
Hair spray	Halogenated hydrocarbons
Non-stick pan spray	Cryofluorane
Pain killing spray	Fluorocarbons
	Vinyl chloride

there are some similarities to the effects of hallucinogens but also to those of alcohol. According to users who also take alcohol, the inhalant gives a much greater euphoria and feeling of omnipotence. Solvents are a popular means of getting kicks because they are relatively cheap and easy to use, the euphoria is almost immediate and there are relatively few unpleasant after-effects. The euphoria lasts for 15–45 minutes after sniffing and ceases when depressant effects such as drowsiness or stupor take over for about 2 hours. After this the person returns to normal.

The above description may give the impression that solvent abuse is a relatively innocuous pastime but this is not the case. The user may suffer serious irritation to the eyes, nose, throat and lungs and, depending on which substance is inhaled, nausea, vomiting, diarrhoea or muscle pains. Some children, when under the influence of solvents, believe that they can fly and some have jumped to their death out of upper storey windows. Reports of terrifying hallucinations are quite common. The stimulating effect can, particularly if the young person is disturbed whilst sniffing, cause fibrillation and sudden death by heart failure. Death whilst inhaling also occurs either from suffocation or from inhaling vomit after becoming unconscious. In 1990 there were 134 deaths resulting from solvent abuse. This seems to be few but they are important in that they represent a disproportionately large percentage of all deaths among males aged 10–14 years.

The first reports of serious long-term physical damage were reported in Bradford in 1969–70 when six youths were found to have liver damage from inhaling solvents. Since then there have been increasingly frequent reports of damage to liver, kidneys and heart. Another very important long-term health risk is that many of the solvents inhaled are known to have carcinogenic (cancer-causing) properties. Although it is too early to be sure, there is also the possibility of long-term brain damage and mental effects similar to those caused by alcohol.

Peer group pressure is a very important factor in the occurrence of solvent abuse which tends to be a group rather than an individual behaviour pattern. Although solvent abuse is found all over the country and in all strata of society, it seems to be more of an urban than a rural problem and is found particularly in deprived inner-city areas. Sometimes the problem is limited to very localised areas such as a single housing estate or even a single school. Often the problem is quite short-lived.

It is extremely difficult to obtain figures for the size of the problem but subjective assessment suggests that the majority of teenagers have sniffed at least once but only a small percentage become regular users. Sniffers have been found as young as 7 years old and the average age for all countries where figures are available is about 14 years. Most have given it up by the age of 18.

Steps have been taken by most governments to make it more difficult for children to obtain solvents but no legislation can prevent the problem. This is partly because the necessary substances are present in all homes for legitimate purposes but mainly because the bulk of abused supplies are obtained by shop-lifting which is the main crime associated with solvent abuse.

Thus, as with other drug problems, whatever legislation and public effort take place the problem will remain. At first, medical authorities were not unduly worried about solvent abuse but as evidence has accumulated, the seriousness of the problem has been realised. Unfortunately, as yet, nobody has been able to formulate a successful way of preventing it. The organisation RESOLV gives help to young people with a solvent abuse problem and also to their families.

Hallucinogenic drugs

4.1 Introduction

Several groups of drugs bring about alterations in perception as one of their major effects. These drugs are variously known as hallucinogens, psychedelic compounds, psychomimetics or fantastica. They belong to several chemically different groups but the majority, the hallucinogens proper, are all **tryptamine** derivatives which are related to the neurotransmitter serotonin (see figure 4.1). A separate group is the **cannabinoids** which are the active agents in cannabis and are dibenzopyran compounds. Included in the hallucinogens is a synthetic compound **phencyclidine** which was produced as a veterinary anaesthetic but is sold on the street as peace pills or angel dust.

All these drugs cause hallucinations which may involve any of the major senses, hearing, sight, touch, taste or smell. Often these senses become confused so that for example colours may be heard or sounds may be seen.

4.2 LSD (lysergic acid diethylamide)

This is the most widely used drug in the group of hallucinogens proper. It was first synthesised by Hofmann in 1938 but he did not discover its hallucinogenic properties until 1943 when he accidentally sniffed some of it. Of the currently known hallucinogens it is by far the most potent, effective doses being measured in micrograms. The drug is misused for its behavioural effects but it also has marked effects on body physiology by influencing the activity of the autonomic nervous system.

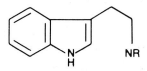

Figure 4.1 The molecular skeleton of tryptamine from which all the hallucinogens proper are derived. R represents the radical which differs in the various substances.

Physiological effects include tachycardia, nausea, tremor, gooseflesh, numbness, muscular weakness and hyperthermia. Tolerance however soon develops and after 3 or 4 daily doses there is little physiological response.

The behavioural effects in humans are a good example of the interaction between pharmacological effects and non-specific factors. Very important in determining the effects are the personality of the user and the setting in which it is taken. The effects begin to appear 20 minutes to an hour after taking the drug and last for between 6 and 12 hours.

One of the common reports by users of LSD is that perception is enhanced, but it is probably more correct to state that it is distorted. Changes in perception in all the sensory fields occur at an early stage of intoxication and after a relatively small dose (less than 20 micrograms). In the visual system, one colour, usually red, green or blue seems to be much brighter than the other colours. New colours which the user cannot accurately describe appear and are often seen swirling around. Any cracks in or bulges on surfaces may be seen as deep cuttings, and folds in a curtain may appear as hills and ridges in a landscape. The walls of the room may seem to slope. People and furniture in the room may merge and split, sometimes seeming to be very large and near, then seeming far away. Distortions in the other senses also occur and become confused so that a colour may be tasted or a sound touched. This crossing of sensory boundaries is known as **synaesthesia**. One possible explanation for these distortions of the environment is that the drug is breaking down perceptual constancies. If one stands in a square room, past experience tells one that it is square but the actual image on the retina is trapezoidal. Similarly, if a room is painted one colour, various intensities are seen, depending on how much light is reflected from various parts. It may be therefore that the LSD user sees the world as it impinges on the retina rather than the normal interpretation of that image. This breakdown of perceptual constancy can be very disturbing for the user as it would not be possible to work out such obvious things as whether a person is small and nearby or large and far away. This explanation of the LSD phenomena means that the drug sweeps away the previous learning of stimulus interpretation and so users have experiences which they think of as perceptual enhancement and feelings of ecstasy. Another suggested mechanism is that LSD opens synaptic connections which are not normally available but there is no substantial evidence for this.

Sometimes, instead of the ecstasy (a good trip) the drug can cause feelings of indescribable terror (a bad trip). Generally the mood change is in the direction of the user's previous feelings and so is connected with the circumstances under which the drug is used. At a pop festival or at a party with friends the likelihood is that a trip will be good, but if someone uses it to alleviate unhappiness then there is a high chance of a bad trip with the person becoming severely or maybe suicidally depressed. Another aspect to the use of LSD is that nobody can be certain of the effects which will occur even if it is being used under favourable circumstances among like-minded companions. Even during a single trip there may be great fluctuations in the mood which occurs.

There seems to be little evidence of acute physiological toxicity to the drug but there are three types of adverse psychological effects, the greatest danger being to those who have borderline mental illnesses before they use the drug.

The first is the occurrence of drug-panic or a bad trip which may give rise to confusion and acute feelings of paranoia which as previously mentioned can lead to suicide. The chance of a bad trip seems to be about 1 in 10 on average but is enhanced by both high dosage and the personality of the user. Usually the effects of bad trips last no more than 48 hours and cause less problem if the affected person is in the company of other experienced users.

The second type of adverse response is that of repeated reactions or after-effects. These are commonly called flashbacks and may occur after either good or bad trips. They may be as short as a few seconds or may last as long as the original trip; they have been reported to occur for up to a year after the last exposure to the drug.

The third type of adverse effect is a long-lasting state of anxiety. This may last for many months and is not easily treatable either by drugs or by psychotherapy. Hospitalisation is often necessary and this treatment may be needed for several months.

Tolerance to and psychological dependence on the drug certainly arise but there is no evidence of physical dependence or abstinence symptoms of a physical nature. Some years ago it was reported that the use of LSD caused chromosome damage and the birth of abnormal babies to mothers who used the drug during pregnancy, but none of these reports has been substantiated by further research. However there are definite dangers in the use of LSD as suicide or semi-permanent mental illness are frequent results of its use. Without doubt it is too dangerous a substance to treat its use as a fad which will run its course, as is suggested by some protagonists.

In the late 1960s and 1970s the street use of LSD was widespread but its use fell off after 'Operation Julie' when the police found the factory producing the bulk of the illegal supplies and broke the distribution network. However the use of LSD is again rising. At present the LSD available in Britain is imported via Amsterdam. In 1990 the street price was £2–5 per unit. The price is lowest in the West Midlands, Liverpool and the Leeds/Bradford area and highest in Glasgow and Edinburgh.

4.3 LSD-like drugs

This group consists of a large number of naturally occurring compounds derived from many different groups of plants and also a number of synthetic compounds. Some of these compounds have been used for religious purposes in South and Central America since prehistoric times and it is possible that the mass psychoses reported in Europe in the Middle Ages were due to the hallucinogenic properties of the alkaloid in the fungus ergot which infects rye.

The best known natural chemicals in this group are:

Mescaline *(3,4,5-trimethoxyphenethylamine)*

Mescaline is the active alkaloid in the **peyote** cactus (*Lophophora williamsii*) and was used for religious ceremonies by the Aztecs, Huichol and other Mexican tribes in pre-Columbian times (before the discovery of the New World). In antiquity the dried button stem of the cactus was eaten but modern abusers may inject the extract. A dose of 200–500 mg produces a hallucinogenic effect for 4–12 hours.

Psilocybin *(dimethylamino ethyl-indol phosphate)*

This is the active agent in **mescal beans** (*Sophora secundiflora*), the use of which preceded that of the peyote, and also of the **magic mushroom** (*Psilocybe mexicana*). The beans were broken open and boiled to make an extract whilst the mushrooms were eaten directly. Structurally, psilocybin is very similar to LSD as are its effects though it is more likely to produce nausea. The effects are felt within about 15 minutes of taking the drug but are of short duration, only lasting 2–5 hours.

STP *(2,5-dimethoxy-4-methylamphetamine, DOM)*

This is a synthetic drug which was probably the first hallucinogen to go directly from the pharmacology laboratory to street use. Among some street users the initials are said to mean serenity, tranquility and peace. It is claimed that trips produced by this drug may last for 3–4 days but such prolonged effects are probably due to contamination with other compounds such as atropine.

DMT *(dimethyltryptamine)*

This is found in **Cohoba snuff** made from the seeds of *Piptadenia peregrina*. It is not an effective hallucinogen when taken orally, but if used intravenously, smoked or sniffed it has effects very similar to those of LSD though they are of very short duration. DET (diethyltryptamine) is a synthetic form of the drug which has, at times, been widely used by hallucinogen-dependent people.

Bufotenine *(dimethyl-5-hydroxytryptamine)*

This is also found in Cohoba snuff and is the psychoactive agent in the **fly agaric** (*Amanita muscaria*). It is not a popular hallucinogen as, at doses which produce the desired effect, there are also severe and unpleasant side-effects due to stimulation of the autonomic nervous system.

4.4 Cannabis

This is one general name for the preparations made from the Indian hemp plant *Cannabis sativa* (see figure 4.2). In street use in the West there are two types of preparation available, both of which have been used by societies in other parts of the world for centuries. Most commonly used is herbal cannabis, that is the dried leaves, stems and flowers. This is **marijuana** which is variously known as boo, bush, fu, gage, grass, griefo, hay, Indian bay (or hay), loco weed, Panama red (a potent grade from Panama), pot or tea. High-grade marijuana is known as Acapulco gold. The second preparation is the resin of the plant which has been pressed into blocks. This is **hashish**, also known as hash or Keif, and is usually prepared from newly fertilised flowers.

Cannabis sativa is a **dioecious** plant, that is it has separate male and female plants. The **pistillate** (female) plants contain more **tetrahydrocan-nabinol** (THC) whilst the **staminate** (male) plants contain little and are grown mainly for their fibre content.

Cannabis is native to the temperate parts of Central Asia but has been grown in the Middle East and in both South and Central America for centuries. At various times it has been used as a source of rope, cloth fibre, bird seed and a medicine. Its essential oils were used legally for medicinal purposes until the mid-1930s. Many of the ancient civilisations from China through India to the Arab world are known to have used cannabis for its intoxicant properties and it is still the acceptable intoxicant in Moslem society which does not allow the use of alcohol. It is also built into the practices of the Rastafarian cult. In the USA a heavy tax was imposed on the use of marijuana in 1937 and this drove its use underground. Since then in the USA there has been anti-marijuana legislation which has been followed by the other Western countries. In 1944 the La Guardia report (*The marijuana problem in the city of New York*) was published, which demolished many of the myths associated with the drug, but this report was vigorously opposed by the American Medical Association and the Federal Bureau of Narcotics. However the users of the drug were aware that the effects of cannabis did not equate with those of heroin with the result that they disregarded all factual information about it as untrue.

The active agents in cannabis are various isomers of tetrahydro-cannabinol, the most active one being delta-9-tetrahydrocannabinol (THC). A 'good' plant from the user's point of view contains 1–1.5% THC. Although the plant will grow almost anywhere (it used to grow on rubbish tips in Britain when *Cannabis* seeds were a constituent of bird seed!) there is much higher THC content in plants grown in the tropics where there is plenty of sunlight and high temperatures.

THC is a fat-soluble substance so it tends to accumulate in body organs such as the liver, lung and testes and there is some research evidence that long-term use may damage these organs. In human lung tissue cultures,

Figure 4.2 The Indian hemp plant (*Cannabis sativa*). Top of female plant and (in background) top of male plant.

marijuana smoke caused more damage than did tobacco smoke. The comparative results suggest that one 'joint' a day has the same effect as a whole packet of cigarettes. This is partly because of a much higher tar content (5 mg per joint compared to 1.2 mg or less per cigarette) and partly because the smoke is inhaled deeper and is held in the lungs for longer. Cannabis use produces a mild tachycardia (palpitations) but does not alter respiration rate or blood sugar level. It has no effect on pupil size but does cause reddening of the conjunctivae and this is one of the surest signs of cannabis use. The reddening is caused by conjunctival vascular congestion. The other physical effect is to reduce the level of body secretions, for example tears and saliva and this effect is thought to be due to the drug blocking the activity of the parasympathetic nervous system. The neurological action of THC seems to centre on the cortical areas of the brain, not the brain stem, and the effects are rather equivocal. Results from animal experiments are not very helpful as there is great variation in the effects on different animals. Also, as yet, research has not produced an answer to how the drug exerts its influence on the brain.

Results from research on the psychopharmacology of THC are also far from satisfactory to date as there is a large discrepancy between the subjective and objective effects on brain function. Users say that they experience major changes in mental functioning and in their state of consciousness, but psychological testing shows little change until tests are made very complex when there is a loss in performance. Unlike the situation with most other drugs, inexperienced users, although becoming intoxicated, often have no mental effects at all. It seems that cannabis smokers can suppress the mental effects or allow them to happen so that the experienced user can increase these effects by his expectation of the result of smoking. One mental effect which is constant with high dosages is the increase in total sleep time accompanied by a reduction in the periods of REM sleep.

In the Western cultures, marijuana is usually smoked but sometimes it is eaten. In the latter situation the effects are more pronounced but are also less predictable. When it is smoked, the effects begin within a few minutes and last for several hours. After inhaling the smoke the user has a feeling of 'inner joy', that is what is usually called a **high**. If alone the user often becomes sleepy but in company is likely to be talkative and hilarious. Sensory perception may be enhanced and there may be changed sensation of space or time. At the end of a trip the user invariably feels lethargic and often feels hungry. Sometimes the drug causes anxiety or slight paranoia, an experience known as a 'bring down' or 'bummer'.

Physical dependence with its consequent abstinence syndrome does not occur with cannabis use but there are reports of psychological dependence developing in some users, particularly those who have other psychological problems or are subject to stress.

In 1990 prices for herbal cannabis ranged from £45–120 per ounce. The extracted resin, which is much more potent as the concentration of THC is higher, costs from £80–120 per ounce. Hash oil which is a diluted form of the resin costs £10–15 per gram. In 1990 it was only available in southern England and the Cardiff area, but it was anticipated that its availability would spread nationwide. MDMA was only available in the London area in 1986 but by 1991 was available throughout the UK.

Many people argue for the legalisation of cannabis on the grounds that it is less harmful than either alcohol or tobacco. However, there is growing evidence that cannabis use may be potentially more harmful to the lungs than is tobacco and there is evidence from countries in the Near East and North Africa, where cannabis is the main socially acceptable drug, that it may be as socially harmful as alcohol. In Britain there are nearly a million people who are physically and/or mentally ill because of the abuse of alcohol and there is good reason to believe that marijuana has the potential to produce a similar problem. At present there are many occasional or controlled users but if supplies were legally obtainable, many of these and also many other people who are at present not involved would be likely to join the small but significant number who are socially and economically maladjusted because of marijuana use. In countries such as Morocco, where cannabis is socially accepted, there are many people, and in Western society there are some, who are constantly dreamy and personally negligent because of constant cannabis abuse. They form the equivalent of the alcohol skid row, these **spaced out** people forming their own sub-culture outside the limits of normal society. There is no evidence from any culture that once a drug has been built into the fabric of society, its use can be abolished at a later date. Our society has very great problems with its legal drugs, alcohol and tobacco, and there is no good evidence that cannabis is a less harmful alternative. In fact it is not, and will never be, an alternative but an addition. Legislation would increase the use of yet another physically and mentally harmful substance and would further enhance the drug problems facing society. The only case for legalisation would be that it was harmless. This is stated by some users but the accumulating research evidence, although to some extent contradictory, is gradually building a case against rather than for the use of cannabis.

4.5 PCP (phencyclidine hydrochloride)

This drug was synthesised in 1957 and was marketed as an anaesthetic. However its use in human surgery soon ceased as in some patients it caused extreme excitement and hallucinatory disturbances. It is still used as a veterinary anaesthetic. PCP is a very dangerous drug with stimulant, depressant, hallucinogenic and analgesic effects, in fact the acute effects are so unpleasant that its popularity is surprising. Originally PCP was taken orally, the usual dose being 2–10 mg. Taken this way the effects are felt after 30–60 minutes and last for several hours. Now it is more common for the drug to be snorted or to be sprinkled on marijuana or parsley and smoked, in either case the effects are felt much more quickly but last for a shorter time.

Moderate doses cause depersonalisation, the user being distanced from his immediate surroundings. Sensory impulses are distorted and body movement is diminished. At higher doses it produces auditory hallucinations and convulsions. Very often, feelings of impending doom or death are produced and the user may begin to behave in a bizarre or violent way. The latter reaction is a result of feelings of power and invulnerability. Depression, anxiety, memory problems and speech difficulties arise from chronic use and there may be long-term paranoia produced.

PCP (phencyclidine hydrochloride)

PCP overdose can produce a life-threatening coma and overdosage is common among users as the strength of the available drug is variable. It is a very popular street drug in the USA (there are an estimated 7 000 000 users) where it is variously known as angel dust, crystal, elephant, monkey dust or scuffle. Some of the workers with addicts in the USA consider PCP to be one of the most dangerous of the abused drugs as it so often causes violent behaviour, long-term psychiatric illness and not infrequently death. As yet PCP is not a major drug problem in Britain but its use is increasing and its ease of manufacture by amateurs is a cause for concern.

F I V E

Opiates and other narcotics

5.1 Introduction

Narcosis is a state of deep stupor, unconsciousness or diminished activity produced by drugs known as **narcotics**. In medicine, the term narcotic refers to any drug that in therapeutic doses diminishes sensibility, relieves pain and produces sleep. In law, and in general use, a narcotic is a drug with properties similar to morphine. Many of these drugs are natural components of the gum produced by the opium poppy (*Papaver somniferum*) (see figure 5.1). The gum is formed by the fruit between petal fall and ripening. In the evening, opium workers use a sharp tool to make shallow cuts in the seed pod and during the night a white secretion oozes out and oxidises to a red-brown gum. The following morning this gum is scraped off and collected as raw opium. Opium is a complex mixture of substances including about twenty **alkaloids** which are basic organic nitrogenous compounds. Three of these are used

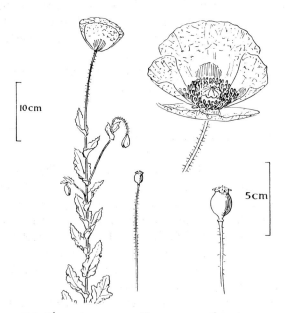

Figure 5.1 The opium poppy (*Papaver somniferum*).

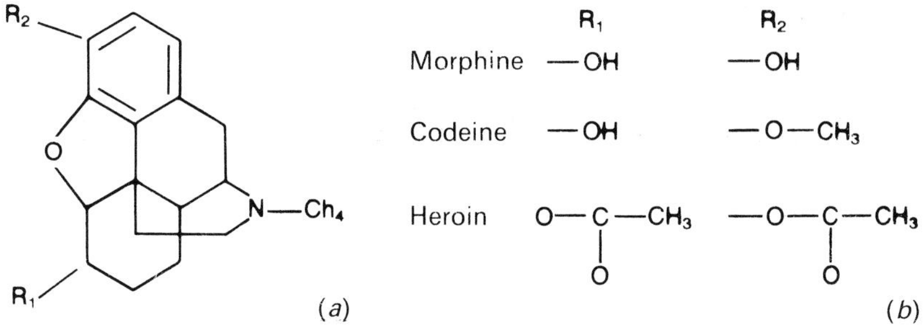

	R_1	R_2
Morphine	—OH	—OH
Codeine	—OH	—O—CH_3
Heroin	O—C—CH_3 (with =O below C)	—O—C—CH_3 (with =O below C)

Figure 5.2 Chemical structure of opiates. (*a*) shows the basic structure of the molecules and (*b*) the radicals (side chains) found at positions R_1 and R_2 in the molecular structure of morphine, codeine and heroin.

therapeutically, **morphine** and **codeine** as pain relievers and **papaverine** as a smooth muscle relaxant. There are also many semi-synthetic opiate drugs which are chemical modifications of the natural products. The best known of these are **heroin** (di-acetyl morphine) and **DF 118** (dihydrocodeine). Finally there are many completely synthetic opiates and related drugs, for example **methadone** (Physeptone), **pethidine** (Demerol) and **dipipanone** (Diconal). All of these drugs are involved in street use, but heroin is the most important. Various slang names are used for it, for example H, horse, Harry, smack or skag.

The 1990 price of heroin varied from £70–120 per gram. An addict may well use $\frac{1}{4}$ g per day or more and so would need £120–250 each week to pay for the addiction. This is why heroin use is so closely associated with many types of crime, from stealing from relatives through shop-lifting to mugging, larceny and burglary. Shop-lifting by young adults is particularly associated with heroin addiction. There are few teenage heroin addicts but occasional use is common among this age group.

As well as heroin, other opiates are commonly misused. At present the misuse of codeine and DF118 are particularly common.

5.2 A brief history of opiate use

Opium has been used certainly since early historic times. There is what appears to be a reference to it on a Sumerian tablet dated about 4000 years before Christ, and the Egyptian papyrus **Ebers** (1500 BC) quotes a remedy for 'excessive crying in children' which is almost certainly an opium extract. It was used in Greek medicine and **Galen**, the last of the great Greek physicians, advocated it almost as a cure-all but also stressed caution in its use. Non-medical use was also prevalent at this time as Galen also refers to opium cakes and candies being sold on the streets.

Comments on opium use appear in writings throughout Europe, the Middle East and Asia during the Middle Ages, the first report of definitely addicted individuals coming from India in the mid-sixteenth century. In the seventeenth century, tobacco smoking was made illegal in China by Imperial edict and tobacco was replaced by opium. A law against opium smoking was passed in China in 1729 whereupon opium smuggling from India became big business. Despite the opium wars (which resulted in Britain being given Hong Kong) opium smuggling continued on a large scale until 1908 when Britain and China agreed to limit imports from India.

The primary active agent of opium (morphine) was isolated in Germany by Serturner in 1806, which started the whole field of alkaloid chemistry. The name morphine was derived from *Morpheus*, the god of dreams. Codeine was isolated in 1832. In 1853, Alexander Wood made a technological advance which was to have a great influence on both the medical and non-medical use of morphine when he invented the hypodermic syringe. As a result of this, combined with the belief that injected morphine would be less addictive than that taken orally, the drug was used as the major pain-killer in the various wars in the late nineteenth century. This addiction idea soon proved to be incorrect and large numbers of returning veterans from these wars were addicted having been given morphine injections to deal with pain or dysentery.

Heroin was first manufactured in 1874 and was originally marketed as a non-addictive replacement for codeine in 1898. The mistake was soon realised but by then heroin addiction was becoming common and has remained the major opiate problem in the Western world ever since. In the USA there is no legal use of heroin at the present time. In Britain, its use is permissible for the treatment of very severe pain in terminal illnesses, though only a limited number of doctors are licensed to prescribe its use.

Illegally used heroin is imported. The origin is largely in the Golden Triangle, the region where Myanmar (formerly Burma), Thailand and Laos meet. At present the main smuggling route to Britain is via the Balkans, but the police expect that new routes will be developed with the opening up of Eastern Europe and the changed political pattern in this region.

5.3 Pharmacology and mode of action

All the narcotics are now known to give rise to physical dependence and consequently an abstinence syndrome when drugs are not available. There is also a psychological dependence which is probably based on the euphoria produced in many users. Morphine is usually treated as the type drug for the group and so a description of the effects of morphine will be given. Table 5.1 shows the relative analgesic effects of several narcotics and the same order of effect applies when they are used for non-medical purposes.

Morphine produces its effects at the synaptic level and seems to work on all levels of the brain from the cortex to the hindbrain. Physiologically there seem to be selective activities: response to pain stimuli is reduced;

Table 5.1 A comparison of the effectiveness of narcotic analgesics

Narcotic	Standard analgesic dose (mg)	Time of onset of peak effect in minutes (subcutaneous injection)	Duration of action (hours)
Morphine	10	30–60	4–5
Heroin	3–4	15	4–5
Methadone	8–10	30	4–6
Meperidine (Pethidine)	80–100	10	2–4
Codeine	120	—	2–4

Note that the time of onset of peak effect is not reduced if the drug is injected intravenously but dosages for the same effect must be higher if the drug is taken orally.

respiratory centres are depressed; hypothalamic response to external stimuli is reduced; nausea is produced by effects on the lower brain centres and pituitary gland function is depressed. Pioneer work by Snyder in the early 1970s identified brain areas that contain many narcotic receptors. Some parts of the limbic system are very rich in them, particularly the **amygdala** and this may be important in the euphoric effects of the opiates. Soon after the opiate receptors in the brain were discovered, several brain **peptides** were found which have morphine-like effects at these opiate receptors. They were given a generic name of **enkephalins**. Since then a more complex molecule has been found in the anterior pituitary which has the enkephalin unit as part of its structure and the name **endorphins** has been coined to refer to all endogenous morphine-like substances. It is now known that the enkephalins are neurotransmitters which are localised in synaptic areas in parts of the brain mediating the integration of sensory information connected with both pain and emotional behaviour, but exactly how they work in normal behaviour and how exogenous opiates have their effects is not known for certain. Two main ideas have been put forward, though neither of them is proven. The first is that when exogenous opiates fill the receptor sites, more receptors are produced. The second is that the presence of exogenous opiate suppresses the production of the endogenous ones. Either of these hypotheses will account for the development of tolerance and also the occurrence of abstinence symptoms when the exogenous opiate is withdrawn.

Opiates also affect many of the other brain neurotransmitters. As tolerance to opiates develops, the synthesis but not the accumulation of **serotonin** increases. This change may in some way be involved in the analgesic effects of the opiates as it is known that a fall in brain serotonin levels increases sensitivity to pain. Changes which may be related to the euphoric effects are increases in the turnover of monoamino transmitters, noradrenalin and dopamine, and an increase in brain levels of acetylcholine.

The effects of morphine are partly due to direct effects on other organ systems. Depression of the respiratory centres makes the breathing slow and shallow and death from respiratory arrest can follow an overdose of morphine. Users have a hypersensitive pupillary response to light and so tend to have smaller pupils than non-users, but the so-called 'pin-point' pupils are only found after overdosing. Morphine stimulates the nausea and vomit centres in the brain and one reason why heroin is more popular with addicts than is morphine is the fact that it has much less effect on these centres. Opiates also have many effects on the gastro-intestinal tract. The secretion of digestive juices is decreased as is the amount of peristalsis. Constipation is therefore common in addicts. Not only does heroin have less nauseous effects but it also produces greater euphoria than does morphine, a fact which also increases its popularity with addicts. It is also more popular with dealers as it is three times more potent, so doses are smaller and more profit can be made.

5.4 Illegal narcotic use

The general pattern is that narcotics users have graduated onto these drugs after using other ones, but at present many young teenagers are being introduced to narcotics as an initial drug experience, particularly in inner city areas. The number of heroin users in Britain is rising all the time with a particularly large rise since 1980. During the past ten years, in the region of 5000 new heroin addicts have been notified to the Home Office each year. The peak was in 1985 when 5930 new addicts were registered. These figures represent the tip of an iceberg as they form only a small proportion of heroin users, most of whom do not register and so do not appear in the statistics. Statistics from 30 years ago suggest that there were very few female heroin addicts but now the ratio is around 3 male to 1 female.

Initially, people take heroin for the euphoria which it produces but for the regular user it often becomes a case of needing the drug to avoid the abstinence symptoms rather than for the pleasure originally experienced, though the two can be combined. Low doses or oral doses will prevent the abstinence syndrome but high doses soon become necessary to produce pleasure as increasing tolerance has to be overcome. High doses are usually obtained by one of two methods. 'Mainlining' or intravenous injection has been the traditional way, but recently a method known as 'chasing the dragon' has become popular. This involves heating the drug on tinfoil and inhaling the fumes.

A common misconception is that mainlining gives an experience of intense pleasure in everyone who does it. There is evidence however, both from research and from street reports, that some people experience only nausea and discomfort and they have to persist until the discomfort decreases and euphoria becomes the main effect. It is also commonly held that after one shot of morphine or heroin you are hooked for life. Perhaps very occasionally this is true, just as there are a few reports of a person becoming an alcoholic after one drink, but for the vast majority, addiction only arises after regular use. It should be remembered though that compared with most other drugs, addiction to heroin does **develop rapidly** and regular use for **one or two weeks** may be sufficient to produce physiological dependence and therefore addiction. Another important point is that it is the regularity of use not the size of the dose which is the initial factor in the development of addiction.

By no means all people who use heroin, even those who inject it intravenously, become addicts. There are many occasional users and others who start and stop at will, but responses to heroin are very varied and no novice user can know whether or not he will become addicted. If a person injects heroin daily then tolerance and so the need to increase the dose can develop very rapidly. 100 mg is a fatal dose for a non-tolerant person, but it is not uncommon for addicts to build up to doses of 500 mg in the space of 10–15 days. When a person stops using the drug either voluntarily or by force of circumstances, such as being in prison, this tolerance is rapidly lost. Many deaths have occurred when people took doses of the size they were using before withdrawal and so took a lethal dose. Lethal doses are also possible with illegal supplies as the users never know to what extent the drug has been **cut** (adulterated by inert substances) and so what actual quantity of heroin they are using.

A further misconception is about withdrawal symptoms. An addict undergoing withdrawal without medical supervision is always shown as being in intense pain and suffering enormously. This is often the case, but there are also many instances where addicts, even some taking very large doses, have few problems when withdrawing.

Although some experts believe that addicts have a constitutional disposition to addiction, others state that environmental and peer group pressures are the most important factors. Availability of heroin is of course a prime factor but the situation now is that, wherever you are in the country, it is available. No communities are without their heroin source. It is very important to remember that people who have not used heroin do not know whether or not they may become addicted and the problems which go with addiction are too great to risk.

For the person who injects heroin there are various health hazards. One of the most important is that street heroin is always impure – it has been cut by the addition of inert substances to increase the dealer's profit. Many different substances are used to cut heroin, including chalk, talcum, soap powder and brick dust. These materials may be injected along with the heroin and give rise to blood poisoning or damage to blood vessels. Often addicts will be injecting in insanitary conditions and be using unsterile needles. This often leads to blood poisoning and abscesses at the sites of injection. Needles may be shared by addicts and this, combined with unsterile technique, can cause serious and often fatal infections such as infective hepatitis and AIDS. Because of the effects of the drug and the fact that any available money is used to purchase it, malnutrition can also be a major health problem.

From the point of view of the individual, the likelihood of addiction and the misery, health hazards and social costs that go with it are very good reasons for not becoming involved in the first place. It may be difficult because of peer group pressures but the safest course is to say no to the first and subsequent offers. From society's viewpoint the social, medical and criminal costs are enormous and increasing efforts are needed to eradicate the drug traffic.

5.5 Withdrawal and treatment

As mentioned previously, the extent to which an addict suffers withdrawal signs and symptoms is very variable, but the sequence is always the same. When people cease using morphine (or heroin) they become anxious and have a craving for more drug after about six hours. Eight hours later, yawning, perspiration, a running nose and tears occur. All of these effects intensify over the next few hours and are joined by pupil dilation, goose pimples, muscle tremors, hot and cold flushes, aching muscles and bones and loss of appetite. Over the next day or so the blood pressure, heart rate, respiratory rate and temperature all rise and are accompanied by restlessness and insomnia. In the last stage of withdrawal which occurs up to two days after the last dose, vomiting and diarrhoea occur causing dehydration and weight loss. Often the sufferer is too weak to stand or sit and lies curled up. Some of these effects can be life threatening, particularly those which result in dehydration, and there is also the possibility of an addict suffocating because of inhaling vomit. The term **cold turkey**, applied to the withdrawal effects, comes from the gooseflesh which appears combined with the shivering. The fact that these withdrawal symptoms are so unpleasant is one of the main features driving an addict to take another dose of the drug as this removes the effects immediately, or if taken soon enough prevents their occurrence at all. Fear of withdrawal is a great motivation for continuance. All these effects are due to a physiological phenomenon known as **rebound hyperactivity**. Body systems whose function has been depressed by the drug become overactive for a period. If the addict can withstand this period and not resort to another dose of the drug the body functions gradually return to normal. Withdrawal under medical supervision is designed to prevent the occurrence of the unpleasant symptoms.

Various methods of treatment have been tried but none of them can boast a high success rate, prevention is much better than treatment. The first stage is always withdrawal under medical supervision and then one or other form of treatment follows. Of the chemical methods, **methadone treatment** is the most widely used. The synthetic narcotic methadone is prescribed as a substitute for heroin. This drug is also addictive but has less euphoric action and people are more able to function socially on a regular dose of methadone than if taking heroin. The theory is that the dose of methadone can be gradually reduced and eventually discontinued, but unfortunately more often than not a permanent methadone addiction is substituted for the heroin addiction. There are some advantages to this treatment however, even if only that the death rate and crime rate are lower for methadone addicts.

The other main chemical method is to give a maintenance dose of heroin. In Britain, addicts can register with a Government agency and obtain narcotics from a clinic to maintain their addiction, but this system though continuing has a very low success rate; addicts more often than not cease to attend the clinics, having gone back to their old habits and companions.

The other main method of treatment is some form of psychotherapy. There are two types of psychotherapeutic group. One is set up by the medical authorities and is either based in or associated with a psychiatric hospital. The others are set up and run by ex-addicts, perhaps the best known of these being Synanon in the USA and, in Britain, Narcotics Anonymous and Families Anonymous. All the groups base their therapy on the need for the ex-addicts to learn a new set of social and life skills. The clients live in a therapeutic group for a period of time and when they leave they can obtain support whenever they need it. Unfortunately the success of these groups is quite low and the majority of ex-members fail to keep out of the drug-using society.

The biology of alcohol

6.1 Introduction

There is a whole series of chemical substances known as alcohols and one of these, ethyl alcohol or ethanol, is the most commonly used and abused drug in Western society. In common speech it is just known as alcohol and this term will be used as a synonym for ethanol.

It is a simple organic molecule consisting of just carbon, hydrogen and oxygen atoms. It is a small molecule (molecular weight 46) with the formula C_2H_5OH. It is very soluble in water, is also fat soluble and only has a weak electric charge so it is easily able to cross cell membranes.

It is formed by the fermentation action of various micro-organisms, usually yeasts, on fruits, cereals or vegetables. The resulting liquid with various additions may be drunk as wines or beers, or the alcohol may be further concentrated by distillation to produce the various spirits or derivatives of them. The approximate alcohol strength of various drinks is given in table 6.1. As shown in table 6.1, the alcohol content of drinks, especially beer and wine, is very variable. Alcohol strength is usually measured in terms of the percentage of alcohol by volume (ABV). In the UK, alcohol intake is measured in terms of units, one unit of alcohol being 8 g. One unit is the approximate amount of alcohol which can be eliminated from the body in one hour. As a general guide this is taken to be the amount of alcohol contained in standard Public House measures which are half a pint of beer (10 fl oz), a glass of table wine (4 fl oz) and a measure of spirits (1 fl oz). However, this is exceeded in a half pint of beer containing 10% alcohol or a measure of spirits containing 35% alcohol. The volume of cans of beer or lager is measured in millilitres (ml). Both the sizes of can and strength of the

Table 6.1 The approximate alcohol strength of various drinks

Drink	% alcohol by volume
Beer, cider	1–8
Table wine	10–22
Fortified wine (vermouth, sherry, port etc.)	18–23
Spirits (whisky, rum, brandy, vodka, liqueurs etc.)	35–50

contents is very variable. For example, a can of lager containing 436 ml with an alcohol content of 5.3% contains 23 g of alcohol, almost three units.

Recommended maximum levels of alcohol intake (see section 7.1) are measured in units of alcohol.

6.2 Absorption and distribution

Because of its small size and chemical properties alcohol is absorbed rapidly from the gastrointestinal tract. It does not need to be digested and its passage is solely dependent on the concentration gradient across the membrane. Taken by mouth absorption begins across the buccal surface, but the first significant absorption is through the gastric mucosa. This is slowed by the presence of food and if the alcohol content of the stomach rises above 10% the rate of absorption is slowed, probably because of its irritant effect on the mucosa. The rest of the alcohol is absorbed through the upper small intestine. Alcohol therefore passes via the hepatic portal vein to the liver and then into the general circulation. It takes time for the liver to deal with the alcohol imbibed and so it is in continuous circulation for a period, the **blood alcohol level** (BAL) rising as long as drinking continues and then gradually falling as the alcohol is metabolised or excreted by the kidneys or lost through the lung surface and body secretions such as sweat. 95% of the absorbed alcohol is metabolised and the rest is lost from the body unchanged.

The BAL produced by a given alcohol intake is variable. Overall body weight is important as the larger a person is, the greater is the volume of blood in which the alcohol is dispersed. A further factor is the percentage of fat in the body. Although alcohol is slightly fat soluble, because there is little blood supply to adipose tissue only a small proportion of the alcohol intake is incorporated into it and so a larger proportion is distributed in the blood and other tissues. A man who weighs 80 kg and who is fat will, therefore, for a given alcohol intake have a higher BAL than a man of the same weight who is tall and muscular. Because, proportionately, women have a higher body fat content than men, for a given alcohol intake a woman will have a higher BAL than will a man of the same body weight. Blood alcohol levels are usually given as milligrams of alcohol per hundred cubic centimetres of blood. Sometimes it is expressed as a percentage of alcohol by volume. The relationship between these two is that 100 mg per 100 cm^3 is equal to 0.1%. Table 6.2 shows the relationship between BAL, sex and body weight.

6.3 Metabolism

The oxidation of alcohol takes place in three stages. The first two are almost entirely limited to the liver, but the product of these enters the energy and

Table 6.2 The relationship between alcohol consumption, blood alcohol level, sex and body weight

Alcohol intake per hour	*Blood alcohol level (mg per 100 cm³)*			
	Female 45 kg	*Male 45 kg*	*Female 90 kg*	*Male 90 kg*
1 oz spirits 〕 1 glass wine 〉 1 can beer 〕	45	37	22	19
2 oz spirits 〕 2 glasses wine 〉 2 cans beer 〕	90	75	45	37
4 oz spirits 〕 4 glasses wine 〉 4 cans beer 〕	180	150	90	70
8 oz spirits 〕 8 glasses wine 〉 8 cans beer 〕	360	300	180	150

Note that these figures are a guide only. The legal limit for driving in Britain is 80 mg per 100 cm³. For a man of 67 kg (10 stone) this is an approximate intake at the 2 level in the table.

anabolic pathways which are common to many tissues. Firstly, alcohol is converted to **acetaldehyde** by the removal of the hydrogen which is taken up by **nicotinamide adenine dinucleotide** (NAD) acting as the hydrogen acceptor. NAD is therefore reduced to become NADH. When alcohol is present in small quantities this process is mediated by an enzyme, **alcohol dehydrogenase** (ADh) found in the cytoplasm of the liver cells. It is possible that some of the alcohol may be oxidised by **catalase** found in the liver cell organelles known as **peroxisomes**. When alcohol levels are high, particularly in the case of chronic alcohol users, a third method of oxidising alcohol to acetaldehyde is brought into play. This is the **microsomal ethanol oxidising system** (MEOS) which is a cytochrome-bound enzyme system. There are two important consequences to the MEOS involvement. One is that the rate of alcohol elimination is increased thus lowering the BAL more rapidly. The second is that the MEOS system also detoxifies other drugs which means that, in the presence of high levels of alcohol, other drugs are removed rapidly. This is one reason why it is unwise to take alcohol when taking antibiotics or similar drugs for treating infections.

The second stage of metabolism is the conversion of the acetaldehyde into **active acetate** by the enzyme **acetaldehyde dehydrogenase**. The

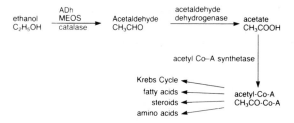

Figure 6.1 The metabolism of ethanol (ethyl alcohol).

active acetate can enter various other metabolic pathways where it is converted by the enzyme **acetyl Co-A synthetase** into **acetyl Co-A** which can be further oxidised in the **Krebs cycle** or be converted into fatty acids, steroids, amino acids and other metabolites. Of the alcohol metabolised, about 85% is oxidised to CO_2 and water via the Krebs cycle and the rest is converted into other metabolic products. The processes involved in the metabolism of alcohol are summarised in figure 6.1.

There are several other metabolic consequences of excessive alcohol intake, largely because of the effect its metabolism has on the NADH/NAD ratio in the body. Because of the increase in NADH, **pyruvate** (pyruvic acid) tends to be converted to **lactate** (lactic acid) and there is a decrease in **gluconeogenesis** (the formation of glucose from amino acids or lipids). In many people this gives rise to **hyperlipaemia**, that is a raised level of lipoprotein, free fatty acid and cholesterol in the blood.

6.4 Central nervous system effects

Although there has been a lot of research, the exact mechanism by which the alcohol affects the CNS is not clear. Most of the evidence points to alcohol acting directly on the neurone membranes rather than at the synapses. The alcohol seems to affect the membrane's ability to generate electrical impulses and so the processing of and response to information is impaired. Although the primary effect is on the membranes, there may also be biochemical influences on the cell function. Acetaldehyde, the primary metabolite of alcohol, is biochemically active and may impair mitochondrial function, protein synthesis and the activity of coenzyme A. It is possible, therefore, that in chronic alcohol users there is impairment of the production of neurotransmitters. Recent research suggests that, as there are specific binding sites for barbiturates and benzodiazepines, there may be similar sites for alcohol. All these sites enhance the inhibitory effect of the GABA pathways. There is also a possible pharmacological link between chronic alcohol use and the processes of opiate dependence. Two groups of researchers have reported the formation of alkaloids similar to morphine as a result of alcohol metabolism. These may well be active at the enkephalin receptor sites in the brain and thus be involved in the development of alcohol dependence.

Whatever the exact biochemical or physiological mechanism, there is a definite and fairly constant sequence of events which accompany increasing alcohol intake. At the lowest level, the **reticular activating system** (RAS) in the brain stem begins to malfunction. This results in the regulation of the cerebral cortex being disrupted and its inhibitory and integrating activity is lost before it is directly affected by the alcohol. Initially alcohol acts as a stimulant. Most researchers hold to the theory that this is because various parts of the cortex, particularly the **frontal lobes**, are freed from inhibition by the depression of inhibitory pathways. However, one researcher has shown that small amounts of alcohol increase electroencephalograph (EEG) activity which suggests that at least some individuals become more alert and active.

Because alcohol impairs the functioning of the RAS, and so indirectly the cortex, there are resulting behavioural changes. At low levels, that is about a BAL of 30 mg %, most people experience a 'high', a sense of well-being. At very low alcohol levels there is no effect, but at some point we become sufficiently uninhibited to 'enjoy' ourselves. Basically this is a situation of impaired judgement but usually it is in circumstances where everyone else around is in the same condition.

It is this initial effect of alcohol that makes it such a popular 'social

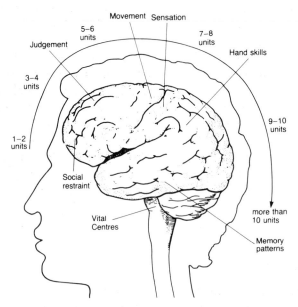

Figure 6.2 The effect of an increasing number of units of alcohol on the brain. Initially the frontal lobes are affected, giving feelings of well-being. As the alcohol intake increases more areas of the brain are affected. More than 10 units will affect the vital centres, leading to coma and possibly death.

Table 6.3 Blood alcohol level and effects on behaviour

BAL (mg per 100 cm³)	Behaviour effects
30	Mild feelings of well-being
50	Lowered alertness, release of inhibitions, impaired judgement, slight unsteadiness
100	Slowed reaction time, impaired motor function, loss of caution
200	Great depression in sensory and motor capability, definite intoxication
300	Stupor and little understanding of the world around them
350	Surgical anaesthetic dose, minimal level causing death
400	50% chance of dying as a result of respiratory depression

lubricant'. Other effects of low doses are the reduction of anxieties because of the disruption of normal critical judgement and, in the case of older people, its anaesthetic effect removes minor aches and pains.

Where further effects on brain function are concerned, it is not only the increase in BAL which is important but also the effect on the brain and so on behaviour. Everyone is affected by rising BAL, but psychological testing suggests that CNS and therefore behavioural tolerance to alcohol does develop. The results show that for equal alcohol intakes the heavy drinker performs better than does the moderate. This may be, but probably is not, due to a higher rate of metabolism in the heavy drinker. Alternatively it may be due to the heavy drinker learning to overcome the disruption caused by alcohol. The sequence of effects with increasing BAL follows the sequence: euphoria, removal of inhibitions, lengthened reaction time, speech difficulties, decreased sensory and motor ability, drunkenness, stupor, death. The relationship of these effects to mean blood alcohol levels is given in table 6.3.

Alcohol-induced brain damage

There is no consensus of opinion as to how alcohol causes damage but some anatomical changes are common among chronic alcohol users, even in many of those who do not show any marked change in brain function. The most noticeable effect is that the brain **ventricles** are enlarged. This may be due in part to excessive loss of brain cells, but the main cause is the shrinkage of cells because of alcohol-induced dehydration. Postmortem examination of the brains of chronic alcohol users suggests that, although there is widespread loss of neurones in the cortex, the major atrophy is in the frontal cortex where there is diffuse and patchy loss of **pyramidal cells**. Apart from the shrinkage of brain cells there is evidence of damage due to **hypoxia** (shortage of oxygen) and **hypoglycaemia** (shortage of glucose) due to the occlusion of blood capillaries by small blood clots. It has also been suggested that an anti-CNS antibody may be formed that would destroy brain cells.

6.5 Alcohol and the liver

Many changes occur in the liver as a result of continued excessive alcohol intake but the most common and important are **fatty liver**, **alcoholic hepatitis** and **cirrhosis**. All three affect both sexes but female livers are more susceptible to serious alcohol damage.

A high alcohol intake puts a great metabolic overload on the liver. The liver prefers alcohol as an energy source and so it ceases to use fat which accumulates in consequence. A secondary effect is that the hydrogen produced as a by-product of alcohol metabolism is converted into more fat, in particular increasing the synthesis of cholesterol and lipoprotein which accumulate as visible droplets in the liver cells. Once alcohol intake ceases, the accumulated fat soon disappears from the liver and for many people there is no permanent liver damage. However, if excessive alcohol intake is continued over long periods there may be permanent liver damage leading to other liver problems.

Alcoholic hepatitis and cirrhosis

Alcoholic hepatitis is the main forerunner of cirrhosis. It is characterised by liver cell damage, inflammation and **fibrosis**, the development of fibrous tissue. Typically the damaged cells are swollen and have wispy cytoplasm with clear areas. This type of damage, if severe will give rise to nausea, loss of appetite, abdominal pain and jaundice. As with fatty liver, the problem is reversible, but if alcohol use continues, the hepatitis becomes increasingly serious and leads to liver cirrhosis. Although this is the most common sequence leading to alcoholic cirrhosis, there is evidence that in some cases there are other factors involved, such as infection with hepatitis B virus. The main anatomical change in a cirrhotic liver is that the liver cells are gradually replaced by fibrous tissue. The liver becomes nodular in appearance and gradually hardens. As liver cells are lost, liver function diminishes and, as a result, much of the body metabolism is adversely affected. Blood flow to the liver decreases, fluid accumulates in the body and jaundice develops. Cirrhotic changes are irreversible but, if drinking ceases, there is no further damage. It is also important to remember that the liver has a large reserve functional capacity and so people can remain quite healthy when suffering from mild cirrhosis.

6.6 Other systemic effects

Although the effects of alcohol on the brain and the liver are the most obvious, most other systems in the body are also affected. Alcohol is taken into the body via the alimentary canal and this tract is directly affected by it. Alcohol in concentrated form (as in spirits) is an irritant and constant exposure to it causes inflammation. The oesophagus may be affected (**oesophagitis**) and chronic **gastritis** (inflammation of the stomach) occurs in about 30% of long-term alcohol abusers. This gives rise to nausea and vomiting, particularly after a drinking bout. There is also a direct effect of alcohol on the pancreas giving rise to **pancreatitis**. The inflammation produced in the gut adversely affects its functioning and, in particular, causes malabsorption of substances that are absorbed by active transport in a healthy gut.

Alcohol also has various effects on the blood and circulatory system. The development of anaemia is very common and the production of both white cells and platelets is affected. Blood cell production is reduced because alcohol is toxic to bone marrow and red cell survival is reduced because maturation of these cells becomes faulty. Alcohol has a direct effect on heart function reducing both the maximum speed and force of contraction of cardiac muscle. These effects reduce the stroke power and also the rise in left ventricular pressure, and so the heart functions less efficiently and the heart rate increases in an attempt to compensate for this. In cases of advanced alcoholism the heart muscle may become fibrous and impregnated with fat. There is also a raised likelihood of coronary heart disease in heavy drinkers when they abstain, but on the other hand moderate alcohol users have fewer heart attacks than abstainers. This effect may be because alcohol dilates the coronary arteries, but it could be that abstainers who have given up alcohol for health reasons are prone to heart disease.

Alcohol affects the activity of the endocrine system, affecting both the hormone secreting glands and the activity of the hormones themselves. Much of this results from alcohol effects on the hypothalamus and pituitary which in turn changes the activity of the other endocrine glands. Many of the changes are biochemically detectable but do not have an overt clinical effect. One of the best-known endocrine effects is that which inhibits the release of **anti-diuretic hormone** resulting in marked diuresis after ingesting alcohol.

Even in Shakespeare's time it was recorded that alcohol increases sexual desire but reduces the performance. As alcohol intakes rise the ability to carry out sexual activity diminishes and in the case of chronic alcoholics reproductory function is often reduced. In males, the sperm count falls and there is often some feminisation. Both of these effects may be due to testicular atrophy, but feminisation can also be due to impairment of liver function. In females, the evidence is contradictory but in some there is a marked reduction in fertility as periods cease.

6.7 Alcohol and nutrition

Nutritional deficiencies are frequently found in chronic alcohol users and it has been suggested that alcohol is the major cause of malnutrition in the Western world.

One gram of alcohol provides 298.2 kJ of energy and so it is relatively easy to provide one's entire energy needs from alcohol alone. However, most alcoholic drinks, and especially spirits, contain few nutrients so deficiencies of protein, vitamins and minerals may occur in alcoholics. Another effect is that although light to moderate alcohol intakes stimulate the appetite, excessive intake leads to anorexia (loss of appetite). This is probably due in part to the ketosis which develops, but also to thiamin deficiencies. Chronic alcohol users often suffer from zinc deficiencies which reduce taste acuity and so indirectly reduce the appetite even further. Nutritional problems for alcoholics are thus caused by poor dietary intake, but matters are made worse by the effects of alcohol on the gut which adversely affect the absorption of any nutrients which are eaten. Chronic alcoholics have deficiencies of most vitamins, but thiamin deficiency is the most common and is very serious as it is the cause of the peripheral neuropathy commonly found and is often involved in the development of Wernicke–Korsakoff syndrome. Deficiencies of nicotinic acid, pyridoxin and vitamin B_{12} also adversely affect brain function.

6.8 Pre-natal effects of alcohol

Alcohol easily passes the placental barrier and so any alcohol taken in by a pregnant woman becomes evenly distributed between mother and fetus. Although none of the effects on fetuses is specific to alcohol there is a progressive increase in minor defects to fetuses and a retardation of growth rate with increased alcohol intake. The occasional drink probably does not matter but there is evidence that regular drinking produces definite risks to the developing fetus. Data suggest that for every 10 g of alcohol taken in daily during pregnancy the risk of developmental anomalies rises by 1.7% and fetal growth is reduced by 1%. It should be remembered that this is a relatively low alcohol intake, equivalent to little over half a pint of beer or one glass of table wine. In the case of women who are chronic alcohol users, and particularly if their own tissues have been alcohol damaged, there is a high risk of severe damage occurring in a fetus. The adverse effects produced constitute **fetal alcohol syndrome**. Growth in the fetus is retarded but particularly in the head, which is small (**microcephaly**), the eyes are reduced and the mid-facial bones do not develop properly. Mild to severe mental retardation is present due to abnormal migration of brain cells and there may be **heart lesions**, particularly defects in the ventricular septum. The most critical stages for adverse effects of alcohol on fetal brain development are in the second month of gestation when the first neural growth takes place and in the last three months when synaptic connection development is taking place.

The adverse effects of alcohol on fetal development have been known for a long time. There are references to it in the Old Testament (e.g. Judges xiii 4) and in Carthaginian writings. Other references appear from time to time, for example a petition to Parliament from the Royal College of Physicians in 1725–6 and a report from a select committee of the House of Commons in 1834. However, fetal alcohol syndrome was not described until 1968 and was not widely recognised until 1980.

6.9 Abstinence syndrome

Because continued use of alcohol gives rise to tolerance and a physical dependence, when it is no longer available to the dependent person an abstinence syndrome develops. Alcohol is a depressant drug and so most of the signs and symptoms of the withdrawal arise from the overactivity of body systems whose function has been depressed. This phenomenon is known as **rebound hyperactivity**. The mildest form is tremulousness which may be an everyday experience for a dependent alcoholic. This arises a few hours after ceasing to drink and so is common on waking and is removed by having a drink. Typically this tremor occurs in the upper limbs and if the person ignores the desire to drink it reaches a peak after 24–48 hours and then subsides over the next 10–14 days. Usually this tremor is accompanied by nausea, sweating and feelings of weakness. A severely tremulous person may also have either auditory or visual hallucinations. A very small minority of abstaining alcoholics develop **alcoholic hallucinosis** where auditory hallucinations occur in a setting of clear consciousness and orientation. This illness is a paranoid psychosis similar to those produced by amphetamines or LSD. The classical case occurs when a person who has been drinking heavily for weeks or months abstains, and voices recognisable as those of family or friends speak to them in a derogatory or threatening way. Fear and distress arise as a response to these threats and may form a basis for secondary delusions.

The serious consequence of alcohol abstinence is **delirium tremens**, but it does not always occur and is very rare in those withdrawing under medical supervision as they are given sedatives, multi-vitamins and anti-convulsant drugs to prevent the syndrome occurring. In delirium

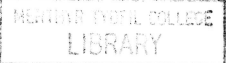

tremens there is persistent tremor of the hands, head and trunk, extreme restlessness and agitation, rapid pulse, fever, sweating and mental disorientation. Visual hallucinations of a terrifying nature always occur and there may also be auditory manifestations. If this problem occurs it is usually about 4 days after the last drink and will last for 3–7 days.

The problems of alcohol use

7.1 Introduction

Alcohol consumption has been present throughout history, probably since the accidental discovery of the fermentation of fruits by wild yeasts.

The use of alcohol is firmly established in society today and whilst it can, without doubt, cause problems, this is not always the case. For most people alcohol is no problem at all. Indeed, there can be beneficial effects of its use in moderation. Small amounts of alcoholic drink can aid relaxation and act as a social lubricant, facts emphasised by its widespread use. There is also some evidence that small amounts of alcohol may protect against heart disease by raising the level of the high-density lipoprotein cholesterol in the blood. However, for a significant number, alcohol can cause serious problems, both to health and to social functioning. Research has shown that there is a level of drinking which is relatively safe and this has been widely publicised in the past decade. For the purposes of this, alcohol consumption has been quantified in terms of 'units'. One unit is defined as 8 g of alcohol, the amount in half a pint of beer or the equivalent quantity of other drinks (see section 6.1). Safe levels of drinking are usually set as up to 14 units per week for women and 21 units per week for men (see figure 7.1). For both sexes it is recommended that 2–3 days per week should be alcohol-free.

The majority of people drink much less than this, but a sizeable minority of both men and women exceed these levels (see table 7.1).

There are, in any society, groups which may be described as **'at risk'**. In the United Kingdom this often relates to those occupations where there is a tradition of drinking and where alcoholic drink is easily available. Among the high-risk group are jobs connected with the licensed trade, theatre and film industry, the Merchant Navy and commercial travellers. The precipitating factor in many of these may be that men are away from their families for considerable periods and that drink is easily, and often cheaply, available.

7.2 Health problems – physical

Although this remains a subject which needs further research it is clear that heavy drinking is implicated in many health problems and puts a

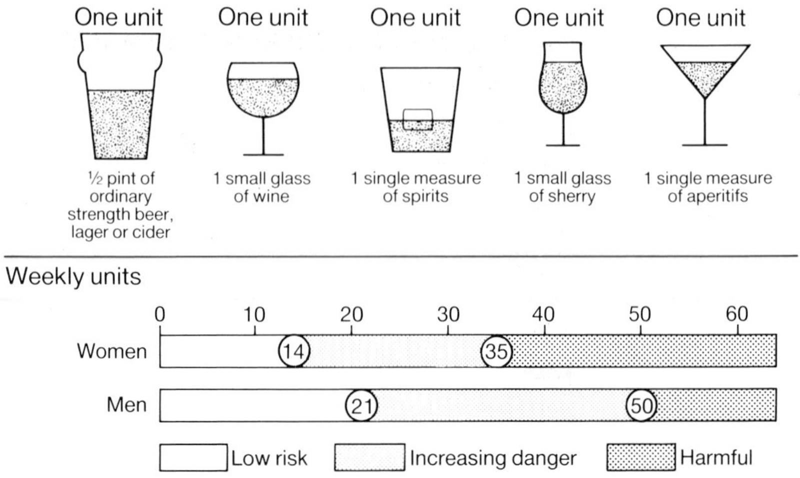

Figure 7.1 Standard drinks containing one unit of alcohol and an indication of harmful weekly consumption for men and women.

Table 7.1 Alcohol consumption, England and Wales, 1988

Quantity of alcohol (units)	Male(%)	Women (%)
None	7	12
Very low (under 1)	10	24
Low (1–10)	35	40
Moderate (11–21)	21	14
Fairly high (22–35)	13	7
High (36–50)	7	2
Very high (51+)	7	1

Data from Social Trends, 1990 (HMSO).

considerable burden on both the general practitioner and hospital services. It is known that men whose drinking problems are severe enough to warrant admission to mental hospitals have a greatly increased mortality rate. As alcohol as a causal factor is rarely mentioned on death certificates it is difficult to be precise about these figures.

Gastrointestinal system

Illnesses of the gastrointestinal system, such as gastritis, pancreatitis and liver damage, can be caused by excessive use of alcohol (see section 6.5). **Cirrhosis** of the liver is the most serious of these. In 1989 there were over 3000 deaths from cirrhosis of the liver in the United Kingdom. Almost

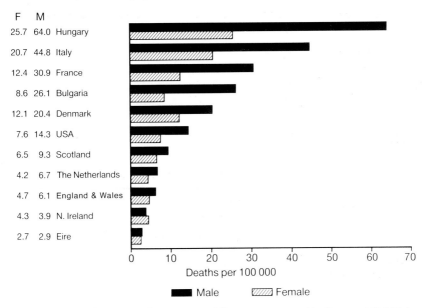

F   M

25.7	64.0	Hungary
20.7	44.8	Italy
12.4	30.9	France
8.6	26.1	Bulgaria
12.1	20.4	Denmark
7.6	14.3	USA
6.5	9.3	Scotland
4.2	6.7	The Netherlands
4.7	6.1	England & Wales
4.3	3.9	N. Ireland
2.7	2.9	Eire

Deaths per 100 000

■ Male   ▨ Female

Figure 7.2 Cirrhosis mortality rates in different countries (deaths per 100 000 in 1986–7).

invariably this occurs in people who have been heavy drinkers for ten years or more. There is a direct correlation between the death rate from cirrhosis and the level of drinking in the population (see figure 7.2). It should be noted, however, that cirrhosis deaths form a relatively small proportion of the overall death rate. Cirrhosis rates vary considerably from country to country but correlate with the overall alcohol consumption in each (see figure 7.2).

Cancer

Recently there has been considerable research worldwide into the relation between cancer and alcohol. It is estimated that 3% of all cancers might be attributed to alcohol. This is quite a small percentage but, as cancer is one of the major causes of death, it accounts for a large number of deaths. The risk of cancers of the mouth and throat in heavy drinkers is more than double that in non-drinkers.

In women there is some suggestion that alcohol is implicated in the causation of breast cancer. Whilst this is not yet fully accepted, if it were the case it would be important as breast cancer is now the commonest cancer in women.

Cardiovascular system

The effects of alcohol on the cardiovascular system have been discussed in section 6.6. Several studies have shown that death from cardiovascular diseases shows a U-shaped curve when related to the level of drinking. The lowest percentage of deaths is in the moderate drinker group and the highest is among the abstainers. This may well be due to people refraining from drinking alcohol when they are ill rather than moderate drinking having a protective effect. It should also be noted that the overall percentage of deaths from cardiovascular causes is much lower (19.4%) among 'alcoholics' compared with 44.5% in the general population. This difference is due to the much higher rate of death by accident in the problem drinkers group. Many of these accidental deaths are road accidents to young men who die before reaching the age to be at major risk of death from cardiovascular causes.

Cerebrovascular system

Stroke is a major health problem causing both disability and death. There is some evidence that the risk of stroke is four times greater in men drinking 30 or more units per week than in non-drinkers. Thus heavy drinking seems to be an important factor in the occurrence of strokes.

Central nervous system

Alcohol damage to the brain may be acute (short term and reversible) or chronic (insidious and largely irreversible). The symptoms are similar in both, the main effects being the loss of short-term memory, the loss of complex intellectual functions, such as calculation, comprehension of information and learning new tasks, and impaired judgement. With chronic alcohol damage there is also confusion and disorientation in time and place. Difficulty is found with tasks requiring verbal abstraction or perceptual motor activity, though there is no overall impairment of intelligence.

Another effect of alcohol on the brain is to produce sleep disturbances. Alcohol reduces the amount of **REM sleep** as it shortens the episodes, though it does not reduce the number of them. Thus it behaves in the same way as other sedative, hypnotic drugs. There is also complete suspension of stage 4 sleep which forms about 20% of normal sleep in young adults. The sleep pattern in young adults becomes more like that in elderly people. Stage 4 sleep is the deep, slow brain-wave part of the sleep cycle. It is also common for sleep to be broken up by frequent waking periods. Overall the sleep pattern of a middle-aged alcohol-dependent person is similar to that of an elderly non-drinker. This has led to the suggestion that the sleep changes may be due to accelerated ageing because of the loss of brain cells. Another possibility is that the alcohol effects may be due to a reduction in brain amines, particularly **serotonin** which is involved in sleep pathways.

Accidents

It is widely accepted that alcohol is a major component in the causation of accidents, particularly in road traffic accidents (see section 7.3). Many people attending Accident and Emergency Units in hospitals, particularly in the evenings (peak drinking time), are found to have a high BAL. A survey in Hull published in 1986 showed that 14% of accident and emergency attendances were alcohol-related. This figure rose to 24% between 8.00 p.m. and midnight and 46% between midnight and 6.00 a.m.

Whilst it is not strictly speaking accidental, cases of injury by assault are frequently alcohol-related. Other accidental deaths which may be attributable to alcohol are caused by fire. Fires may happen when people who have been smoking and drinking fall asleep without extinguishing cigarettes. Some cases of drowning have also been related to a high BAL.

7.3 Health problems – psychological

Minor problems

Over-indulgence in alcohol frequently leads to minor, short-term problems which are experienced by a very large number of people, many of whom cannot be classified as problem drinkers.

Intoxication
Mild intoxication usually leads to a sense of well-being and relaxation. However, this can easily lead to further consumption and the less-acceptable effects of intoxication. It is now believed that, up to a point, the results of intoxication are culturally determined and, in Western culture, the results tend to be aggressive and irresponsible behaviour.

Amnesia
Alcohol-related blackouts or the inability to remember recent events, particularly those associated with the drinking episode, are very common. About a quarter of all men have experienced one.

Hangover
Hangover is a complex state containing both physical and psychological symptoms. The physical symptoms include loss of appetite, nausea and headache. The psychological symptoms may include feelings of guilt and misery and a resolve (often soon forgotten) to drink more moderately in future. It is now thought that minor withdrawal symptoms may play a part in hangover.

Alcohol dependency

Whilst many people who drink alcohol in quite large amounts have complete control over their drinking, there are others for whom alcohol dependence becomes total. There are over 500 000 people in the UK who have a serious drinking problem.

The development of alcohol dependence follows a fairly typical progression. This usually starts with a tendency to drink more quickly than others and, in company, to be the first to get a second drink. Drinking then occurs more often and for longer periods at a time. This is followed by the development of strategies to get more drinks or to sneak drinks unobserved. A need to drink in order to perform adequately at work or socially soon develops and drink becomes a necessity. At this stage guilt feelings may occur but are not expressed.

As drinking develops into dependence and control is lost, life becomes dominated by alcohol. Relationships in both the family and work situation deteriorate. Financial problems arise as an increasing amount of money is spent on alcohol and this can further increase the family tensions. Physical deterioration occurs. The **abstinence syndrome** leads to morning tremulousness (the shakes) and thus to morning drinking, often with supplies of drink being hidden. Often meals are neglected and general health becomes worse. Socially, employment may be lost and marriage breakdown occur.

For many years this was known as **alcoholism**. Probably its best-known definition is that which was produced by the World Health Organisation in 1952.

> Alcoholics are those excessive drinkers whose dependence on alcohol has attained such a degree that they show a noticeable mental disturbance or interference with their bodily or mental health, their interpersonal relations and their smooth economic functioning, or show . . . signs of such development. They therefore require treatment.

This was followed by a period in which help was made available, to a large extent through the psychiatric services. Treatment was often linked to a lengthy stay in a mental hospital. This had the effect of deterring some people from seeking help. Its success rate was not very high, about one-third made a good recovery, another third improved but were unable to stop drinking and the remaining third did not respond to treatment.

More recently there have been moves to relinquish the illness concept and the 'medical model' of treatment. This has been replaced largely by a wider view and the concept of alcohol-related problems of which dependency is one. Help is now more likely to be offered in terms of a problem-solving approach. The terms 'alcoholic' and 'alcoholism' are now little used.

Long-term effects

There is a wide spectrum of neurological impairment (brain damage) related to alcohol use. This ranges from poor coordination and slowness in problem-solving, which may occur in quite young heavy drinkers, to a form of dementia known as Korsakoff's syndrome (see section 11.1) which includes disorientation and memory loss.

7.4 Drink and driving

Drink–driving is a major problem in most Western countries. A breath test is standard procedure in most, the main difference being the level of alcohol in the blood at which driving becomes illegal. In Britain the legal limit for driving is 80 mg per 100 cm³ of blood, but the level is lower in many other countries and in some it is illegal to drive with any alcohol at all in the blood. There is a relationship between the amount of alcohol found in the breath with that in the blood and also in the urine. The roadside test carried out by the police is the **breath test**. If a person is found to have a positive breath test, this is followed up by a test of the alcohol level in the blood. A person may opt for a urine test instead of a blood test. The legal limit of 80 mg% blood alcohol level has the following equivalents, 107 mg% in the urine and 35 μg (micrograms) in the breath.

Breath testing

Under the present law the police may carry out a breath test:

a when they suspect a driver has been drinking;
b when a moving traffic offence has been committed or is suspected;
c when an accident has occurred.

The 1972 Road Traffic Act empowers the police to stop vehicles and they may then decide whether or not there are grounds for requesting a breath test.

As the years have gone by the number of breath tests carried out has increased, but the percentage of positive tests has decreased. In 1981, 163 900 tests were carried out and 38% of them proved positive. In 1989, out of 492 500 tests carried out only 19% were positive.

Alcohol and road traffic accidents

The number of drivers and riders killed in road traffic accidents who were over the legal limit fell between 1981 and 1989 from 28% to 21%. These figures are consistent with other indicators that drink–driving is decreasing, but there is no room for complacency. The figures indicate that at least 1 in 5 fatalities resulted from accidents where one or more drivers or riders were over the legal limit. It is also estimated that 1 in 10 of all non-fatal casualties (25 000) people got their injuries in drink–drive accidents.

It must be remembered that accidents involving drivers who are above the limit do not only kill themselves but may also kill or injure passengers and drivers of other cars involved, or pedestrians, who have not been drinking. Some of the most significant of these deaths occur when a driver who is over the limit crosses over the central reservation of a motorway and has a head-on crash with a vehicle coming in the opposite direction.

The numbers of failed breath tests and the number of drink-related accidents are lowest in the morning and reach a maximum just before midnight. There is also variation throughout the week. The number of fatal accidents which are drink-related are three times higher on Friday and Saturday nights than on other nights in the week.

It should be noted that it is not only drivers under the influence of drink who are involved in accidents. Many pedestrians killed in accidents have a high BAL and this is probably a factor giving rise to the accident. Figures suggest that between 10 p.m. and 4 a.m., 70% of the pedestrians killed who are over the age of 16 have a high BAL.

The risk of an accident and alcohol levels

There is a cumulative risk of being involved in an accident as the BAL increases. It must be remembered that 80 mg% is the *legal* limit for driving, not the *safe* level.

Alcohol interferes with muscular control, decreases alertness especially in the dark, increases reaction time and impairs the ability to judge speed or to deal with the unexpected. All these effects impair the ability to drive safely. As alcohol also impairs judgement, many people feel that they can drive better when they have had a drink.

Several studies have shown that the likelihood of having an accident increases as the BAL increases. This is shown in figure 7.3.

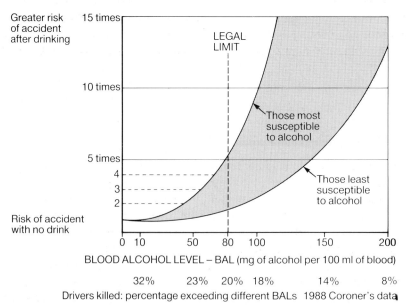

Figure 7.3 The effect of the increasing blood alcohol level of drivers on the risk of road accidents (adapted from *Alcohol can damage your health*, Alcohol Concern 1991).

64

A very detailed study was carried out by the police in Indiana in 1964. They measured the BAL of every person who had an accident during the study period. Then control information was obtained by stopping people at the same points on roads and taking their blood alcohol measurements. The results showed that at 80 mg% the accident risk was double the sober risk and at 150 mg% it was increased ten times.

Studies of drink–drivers

Several studies have been carried out and records are also kept by the Driver and Vehicle Licensing Centre. Although the findings differ in detail, there is an overall pattern. The greatest incidence of drink–driving offences occurs among male drivers in the 20–9 age group. This group accounts for two-fifths of the offences but one-quarter of the licence holders. 40% of licence holders are women but they only account for 5% of offenders. Another feature is a correlation between offenders found guilty of drink–driving and guilty of other traffic offences such as careless or reckless driving. The Nottingham Accident Study in 1988 also showed a high incidence of licence offences among those found guilty of exceeding the legal alcohol limit. Of those with a high blood alcohol, 11% had no valid licence compared to only 1% of those with a low blood alcohol. Similarly there were more provisional licence holders among the high alcohol group than among the low group.

Results of roadside surveys in both Sussex and Warwickshire showed that 44% of those over the limit thought that they could drive safely at the legal limit but only 10% of the sample as a whole thought that they could. It was also found that a higher percentage of those over the limit thought that they could drink 5 units of alcohol or more and still be under the legal limit.

7.5 Social problems

Drunkenness and crime

Drunkenness is not of itself an offence and so statistics about it are very inaccurate. The quoted figures refer only to those found guilty of a related offence and so represent only a small proportion of the people who become intoxicated. The figures do, however, show a downward trend with less than half the number of cautions or convictions in 1989 than in 1981 in England and Wales and a fall of about 25% in Scotland.

Those who appear before the courts on drunkenness charges are mainly either drunk and disorderly or drunk in a public place, in other words they are creating a public nuisance. Although the overall number of cases has fallen, the proportion of young adults involved has increased. This has led to the coining of a new term, 'lager louts', referring to young people who drink large amounts of alcohol and then engage in antisocial behaviour, usually aggressiveness towards other people and destruction of property.

The other groups appearing in court are those involved in crime in which drink has played a part. For example, drink is involved in the behaviour patterns of about 60% of petty recidivists, the group which forms a large part of the prison population. For drunks who are dependent on alcohol other crimes become important, for example fraud or larceny which are used as a means to finance the drinking.

Drunkenness is also involved in more serious crimes; for example, it is a causative factor in more than 50% of wife-battering. Drink is also responsible for many violent crimes outside the family, for example sex assaults on children, sadistic rape and grievous bodily harm. Although there is this relationship between the crimes and heavy drinking, one cannot say that the crimes are actually caused by the heavy consumption of alcohol.

Apart from those who appear in court on drunkenness charges many more become drunk, some quite frequently, but at home or in other social situations where no public nuisance is caused and there is no police involvement.

It is very important to remember in this context that the majority of those who get drunk do not have an alcohol dependence or any compulsion to drink. Similarly the majority of those who are alcohol-dependent seldom, if ever, get drunk. Drunkenness and alcohol dependence are two separate problems and only occasionally do they affect the same individual.

Financial and economic problems

Problem drinking can lead to major financial problems at a personal level. As dependence on alcohol increases, an increasing proportion of the income is spent on drink, particularly when spirit drinking is involved. This, in itself, can cause serious difficulties but, when drinking also leads to the loss of a job and consequent loss of income, the problems may become insurmountable. Default on hire purchase or mortgage repayments may occur with, in some cases, repossession leading to the loss of the family home.

In economic terms one must also consider the cost to the country. This is almost impossible to quantify, but includes the amount spent by the Health Service, Social Security and Social Services and also time lost to industry in reduced productivity and absenteeism.

Personal relationships

As has been mentioned above, heavy drinking can cause considerable stress to a family. Money spent on alcohol and time spent in drinking can cause feelings of neglect. Intoxicated behaviour causes embarrassment and may lead to social isolation from friends and neighbours. Violence in marriage, which is a cause of marital breakdown, is often cited by 'battered wives' as being alcohol-related.

Child neglect and abuse

Heavy drinking has long been recognised as featuring in child neglect, particularly in single-parent families or where the mother is a heavy drinker. Instances of children being left to fend for themselves outside public houses go back to Victorian times. These, together with cases of children being left unattended at home whilst parents are out drinking, still occur. So also do instances of parents drinking heavily in the home, thus rendering themselves temporarily unfit to have the care of small children. Physical abuse can occur as a result of aggressive behaviour due to drink.

Child abuse may also be alcohol-related. A study by the NSPCC between 1977 and 1982 showed that heavy drinking was a factor in 20–25% of reported child abuse cases. A survey of sexual abuse of children in the USA showed that 49% of offenders were drinking at the time of the offence and 34% were heavy drinkers. Sexual abuse has also been known to occur when a wife resists the sexual advances of a drunken husband who then assaults his daughters.

Prevention and control of alcohol problems

8.1 Introduction

The number of people whose drinking is above safe limits, in other words the people for whom drinking causes problems, is related to the proportion of the population in any society who drink alcohol. These problems are many and varied, and it is therefore in the interests of both the individual and the state that some attempt is made to control consumption and thus minimise the problems. This can be approached in different ways, by controls which emphasise the disadvantages of drinking and by education which enables people to understand more about alcohol and hopefully exercise a greater control over their own drinking.

8.2 Availability and licensing laws

Prohibition would seem to be the ultimate and obvious solution. In some Moslem countries there are prohibition laws with severe penalties for infringement. They operate with a fairly high degree of success, but this is probably because alcohol is forbidden by religious law. In countries where drinking is common and there is no widespread religious opposition, similar legislation has never been effective. In the USA the Prohibition Law of the 1920s was unpopular and in fact triggered a wave of organised crime with the gangster syndicates importing and distributing liquor. This law was repealed in 1933 because it was unworkable.

A more realistic approach to the control of consumption is to restrict the hours during which alcohol may be sold, that is by imposing licensing hours. In the United Kingdom these were first used, with some success, during the First World War, following a high level of drunkenness in munitions workers which had resulted in a shortage of armaments for the fighting services.

Laws regulating the availability of alcoholic drink have been used in a variety of forms since then. These have included restrictions on where, when and, by imposing an age limit, to whom alcohol may be sold. The licensing laws were amended in England and Wales in 1988. This change removed many of the restrictions on opening hours and allowed for all-day opening of public houses. However relatively few establishments have taken advantage of the opportunities for all-day opening.

It is difficult to be sure about the overall effects of this easing of restrictions. So often statistics can be misleading as more than one factor can affect changing patterns. The sale of alcoholic drink in this country comes under two classes of licence: 'on licences', where alcohol is sold for consumption on or off the premises and 'off licences' where alcohol is sold to be consumed only off the premises.

At the same time that the licensing laws changed, the number of outlets for alcohol, such as grocers' shops and supermarkets, increased. An increase was also seen in the number of women both purchasing and consuming alcohol. These factors can combine to make it difficult to relate any change in consumption to increased pub opening hours.

There is evidence that changes which make alcohol more easily available often result in a short-term increase in consumption, but it is difficult to estimate the long-term effects.

8.3 Drunkenness and drink–driving – legislation

Drunkenness in itself is not an offence. The legislation relating to drunkenness applies where drunkenness becomes a public nuisance. Charges which can be brought are drunk in a public place, and drunk and disorderly. A significant number of drunks who are apprehended are dealt with by a police caution rather than being taken to court.

At the present time, drink–driving offenders do not lose their licences until they have been found guilty in a court. This may not happen until 10–12 weeks after the offence has taken place allowing plenty of time for the offence to be repeated. In 1991 the Royal College of Physicians recommended that the law be amended so that drivers accused of drink–driving cannot drive between the time of the alleged offence and their court appearance. This would not be necessary if the delay in hearing these cases could be minimised and there is considerable pressure for this to happen.

8.4 Fiscal and economic controls

Taxation plays a major part in the cost of alcoholic drink. The objectives of a taxation policy are not, however, restricted to the limitation of the damage caused by alcohol. They also include the generation of revenue, the protection of the drinks industry and the control of the cost of living (alcohol is included in the commodities on which the **Cost of Living Index** is calculated). Increases in the taxation of alcohol over recent years have tended to be in line with inflation. These increases usually result in a very short-term reduction in the purchase of alcohol.

At present **excise duty** accounts for 40% of the cost of beer and wine and 60% of the cost of spirits. Wine used to be taxed at a higher rate than beer, but this was lowered in response to a European Court ruling in 1983. There are further moves within the European Community towards a common policy for taxation of alcoholic drinks. If this happens the effect will be to reduce taxation, particularly on wine. The likely effect of such a change could be a dramatic increase in alcohol consumption in this country with a resultant rise in alcohol-related problems.

Excise duty is only one part of the cost of alcoholic drink. Any limitation of consumption is governed more by the 'real' cost or the percentage of income spent. When all factors are taken into consideration, the 'real' cost of alcoholic drink is now down to half of that in the 1950s, and consumption is similar to that in the 1900s when the Temperance Movement was at its height (see section 9.1).

8.5 Education and publicity

Whilst the state can and must take some responsibility for controlling the consumption of alcohol by its citizens, this is not the only form of control which is either necessary or desirable. The individual must also take responsibility for his or her consumption. To enable people to assume responsibility they must have enough information to make an informed choice about their own actions.

Although in recent years there has been more information available about alcohol and its effects, it is not enough just to give people broad general information, more detail is needed. The widespread dissemination of information about safe levels of drinking in terms of units of alcohol has been a big step forward, but this does not go far enough. There is considerable variation in safe levels from individual to individual. It is not only gender which governs safe amounts. The rate at which alcohol can be metabolised depends to a large extent on body water content which is related to body size, another relevant factor in estimating an individual's 'safe' level. This, together with other factors which affect a person's susceptibility to alcohol, must be taken into consideration. Whilst the concept of an acceptable unit consumption per week is very useful, it should not be regarded as infallible.

To make an informed choice of how much we should drink we need fairly precise information. The interpretation of safe units is not always easy. Although the figures quoted are given on 'standard measures', these can be confusing. For a start, beers tend to be sold in imperial measures (pints) and wines and spirits in metric measures (litres). Drinking beer or spirits on licensed premises one can be fairly sure that a measure is standard, but glasses of wine tend to vary in size. Due to the variation in packaging, alcoholic drinks bought for consumption away from source can be very confusing. With different sizes and shapes of containers and also promotional packs with '10% extra free' etc., it is very easy to underestimate the amount of alcohol contained.

Since 1989, following an EC directive, alcoholic drinks must state the alcohol-by-volume content on their labels. Although this is useful information, it does not give a precise indication of the amount of alcohol contained (and the alcohol content of drinks can and does vary considerably). Units of alcohol show much more clearly the amount of alcohol contained and thus consumed. At present, the concept of units of alcohol is not commonly used in Europe. However, in the UK the Health Education Authority is supporting the use of units as an effective way for people to monitor their alcohol intake.

The alcohol industry itself can help here. One way in which they have done this is by the introduction of **low-alcohol** beers and wines. This has helped a little to keep consumption down whilst not limiting sales. They could also help by putting more information on labels. A promising start was made in 1991 by Tesco who started to label their own-label drinks with the number of units per 125 ml glass.

A control of consumption has also been attempted by control over the advertising of alcohol products. The British Medical Association would like to see a ban on the advertising of alcohol. This was done in a limited way many years ago in the case of the tobacco industry by the banning of cigarette advertising on television and the inclusion of a health warning on all packets of cigarettes. The alcohol industry would argue that the purpose of advertising is not to influence a desire to drink but to influence brand choice.

The Independent Broadcasting Authority which governs advertising on radio and television has a statutory Code of Practice, and the Advertising Standards Authority which covers newspaper, magazine and poster advertising has a voluntary **Code of Practice**. These do not allow the advertising of drink to be directed towards young people (actors under 25 cannot appear in drink adverts), or to allow drinking to be associated with sexual gratification or prodigious physical feats. Although these are good, they are not always adhered to completely.

Another area which raises questions is that of sports sponsorship. Whilst sports sponsorship is to be commended, there are some associations between the sponsoring and the sponsored which seem inappropriate and the industry has now withdrawn from sponsoring motor racing. There remains at present a major ocean yacht race where both the race itself and the recent winning yacht were sponsored by breweries. Questions have also been raised about the appropriateness of both advertising at football matches and the sponsorship of football teams by the alcohol industry in view of the link between drinking and football hooliganism.

Although informed choice must be a personal matter, whether or not it

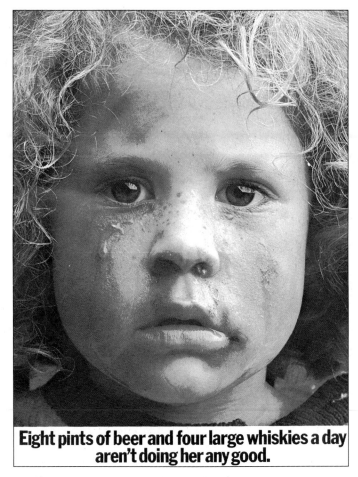

Eight pints of beer and four large whiskies a day aren't doing her any good.

Figure 8.1 A poster produced by the Health Education Authority.

is influenced by advertising, there is a part for society in general to play in making available the information on which to base such a choice. This has been attempted in many ways. One such has been the concentrated campaigns at Christmas aimed at drink–driving. It is difficult to assess the success of such campaigns but there is no evidence that they have been very successful, nor that they have a long-lasting effect.

To change attitudes to drinking will not be easy. The consumption of alcohol is firmly established in our culture. It is closely linked with the concept of hospitality and with celebration. It is also closely linked with the idea of manliness. Whilst today's realistic aims would be to advocate moderation and control rather than the Victorian ideal of total abstinence, they will not be achieved easily or quickly.

The need is to change attitudes, not to modify short-term actions. This can best be achieved by good **health education**, both of young people and

Figure 8.2 Another poster produced by the Health Education Authority about the safe limits of alcohol intake.

of older drinkers. Teachers and youth workers need to be better informed about alcohol-related topics. An awareness of alcohol and its problems should be integrated into the whole curriculum, along with information about smoking, drugs, healthy eating and life-style. Sports, pop music and radio or television personalities can sometimes have a very positive role to play here.

The education of the general public poses rather different problems, but is becoming easier as people become more aware of what makes a healthier lifestyle. The first real attempt to educate the public was undertaken by the Tyne–Tees alcohol education campaign which ran from 1974–84. It was run by various professionals (doctors, staff from alcohol treatment agencies and health education officers) and included training for field workers and education for the public through radio, television, exhibitions, talks and workshops. The high-profile campaign was generally felt to be a success and generated a demand for help from the specialist alcohol services.

Since then there have been a series of **Drinkwise** events aimed at making facts about alcohol and its effects widely known and promoting sensible drinking. Since the first Drinkwise Day in London in 1986 these have become annual national events, with intensive publicity supported by local radio and television. They do not attempt directly to prevent drinking or reduce harm, but to make everybody aware of the importance of understanding their own limits of sensible drinking.

The Health Education Authority have produced a good range of posters both giving information about safe alcohol intake and also relating alcohol misuse to other social problems (see figure 8.1). One of the problems of increasing awareness of alcohol and its related problems is the cost of health education. At present the budget made available for this is very small. Health education rarely shows immediate results and must be seen as a very long-term exercise. It will be a long time before attitudes change and drinking is reduced, and an even longer time before the effects of such a change bring about a drop in the cost of alcohol misuse. However, progress is being made. There are two signs of this, drink–driving is diminishing and more people are seeking help earlier for alcohol-related problems.

NINE

Help for problem drinkers

9.1 Introduction

Although the consumption of alcohol has probably caused problems throughout the ages, it is only relatively recently that any help for problem drinkers has been available. The first evidence of this was during the Victorian era of very heavy drinking, with the development of the **Temperance Movement**. This was really aimed at total abstinence. It was then that the term '**teetotal**' was coined, deriving from a campaigner with a speech defect who had difficulty in saying the word 'total'. This Movement was linked with the more evangelical branches of the church who preached salvation from the 'demon drink'.

In the 1930s a more positive form of help was started by the self-help organisation **Alcoholics Anonymous**. This was followed much later in the 1960s by the development of treatment facilities within the psychiatric services. The approach nowadays is for a wider and more flexible range of help to be provided by voluntary organisations and the health services working together.

At the national level the formation of the charity **Alcohol Concern** in 1984 has done much to further the cause of reducing harm from alcohol misuse. It has been a valuable resource in the promotion of information about alcohol, in supporting local agencies who are both working to help problem drinkers and providing a wide-ranging, integrated service.

9.2 Sources of help

Self help

Self help has always been in evidence and, over the years, some problem drinkers have been able to solve their problems with little or no outside assistance. This has been helped in recent years by the improvement in the alcohol education programmes which have become available. More people are able to help themselves by learning about dangerous levels of drinking in time to control their drinking before the problems become insurmountable.

The organisation of **Drinkwatchers Network**, which was set up by the charity **ACCEPT** and was rather like Weightwatchers, has also been a useful self-help resource. Their Drinkwatchers Manual, which was given to everyone attending one of their meetings, proved helpful to people with an early or potential drink problem.

However, without doubt, the most significant self-help organisation is **Alcoholics Anonymous** (AA). This was started in the USA in 1935 by two men with severe drinking problems and is now thought to have more than a million members throughout the world. It remains a self-help organisation, neither seeking nor accepting funding from outside. AA aims at total abstinence for its members. Their philosophy is that of admitting the power that alcohol has over them and through a spiritual awakening to a commitment to help other 'alcoholics'. They work through local group meetings where members are known only by their forenames and at which they talk openly about the problems which alcohol has caused them. With mutual support their aim is not to drink 'today'. Although there is an emphasis on spirituality (reliance on a higher power) which deters some people, AA does not require or preach any religious belief.

Many people with severe drinking problems find that the opportunity to start a new social life in a non-drinking environment is very helpful. However, although AA has helped innumerable people, its approach does not suit everyone. It is perhaps less helpful to people in the earlier stages of problem drinking.

There are also two self-help organisations allied to, but independent of, AA. These are **Al-Anon**, an organisation for the families (more usually wives and girlfriends) of 'alcoholics' and **Al-Ateen** helping their teenage children.

Statutory agencies

Many of the statutory bodies play a part in helping people with alcohol-related problems. These include the **Probation Service** which becomes involved because of the relationship between crime, particularly petty and recidivist crime, and alcohol. Many probation officers have an interest and considerable expertise in counselling problem drinkers. They may also become involved in helping to find hostel or other residential accommodation for homeless problem drinkers. **Social Service Departments** also have problem drinkers amongst their clients in their work with child care and family problems. However, with all the other pressures on these departments, most of them give a fairly low priority to work with problem drinkers and tend to offer help by referral to specialist agencies.

The **Health Services** are the statutory services which have the major role in helping those with alcohol-related problems. Their contact with problem drinkers occurs in many ways. As it is known that people with a drink problem contact their general practitioners more often than the average person, this may be the first opportunity for help to be offered. It is very easy for this opportunity to be missed, but fortunately there is now a greater tendency to include questions about drinking habits when taking a general medical history. As this becomes more widespread, early diagnosis of alcohol misuse should become easier, leading to the availability of counselling either in the Health Centre itself or elsewhere.

The Health Services major involvement with problem drinkers comes through its mental health services. With the trend towards care in the community and the closing of in-patient facilities, there has been a move towards help for problem drinkers being community based and to the development of **Community Alcohol Teams**.

For many years, treatment for problem drinkers was provided by admission, usually for between 6 and 12 weeks to a specialist **Alcohol Treatment Unit**. Partly because of the general trend towards community care and partly because the results of treatment on these units did not seem to justify the expense, many of them have now been closed and their resources transferred to a community service. There do, however, remain some problem drinkers, both those whose drinking has reached a level where they need more intensive care or those whose drinking is linked with another form of mental illness, who still need admission to psychiatric hospital. **Detoxification** is often done on an in-patient basis. This comprises the control of withdrawal symptoms by a regime of sedative drugs, anti-convulsant drugs and multi-vitamins. Detoxification is now sometimes carried out at home, but this is dependent on family care being available and on regular monitoring by the general practitioner and a community psychiatric nurse.

Voluntary agencies

The major role of voluntary helping agencies has developed over the past 20 years and many of them have an invaluable expertise. They include non-specialist agencies who deal with alcohol-related problems as secondary to their main function and specialist agencies who exist to help the problem drinker.

The non-specialist agencies include the **Samaritans** (a telephone counselling agency which aims to help those who are in despair or who are suicidal) and **Relate** (formerly the Marriage Guidance Council). Both of these organisations find that drink problems feature significantly in their referrals. The **Salvation Army** is also involved in helping those with drink problems. Traditionally they have helped the lower strata of society and currently are providing hostel accommodation for many homeless people whose problems are linked to alcohol misuse.

The main specialist agencies for helping those with alcohol-related problems today are the **Alcohol Advisory Centres** or local **Councils on Alcohol**. They started to develop in the early 1970s. In the early days they provided a service for the less well-motivated drinkers who were not served by the Alcohol Treatment Units, providing Drop-in Centres with coffee and counselling as an alternative to drinking in pubs. They have developed to provide a comprehensive service in both alcohol education and counselling. Although they are voluntary bodies (usually registered charities) they do not attract much in the way of donations from the general public and are largely financed by grants from statutory bodies, including the Department of Health, local Health Authorities and Local Authorities (through Social Service Departments). They have both paid staff and volunteer helpers.

Other specialist agencies which play a part in helping are those organisations which provide residential accommodation and rehabilitation for the homeless or people who need time out from their usual environment. These include the charities **Turning Point** and **Aquarius** (which operates largely in the Midlands).

9.3 The integrated approach

The Kessel Report, published in 1978, in making recommendations as to the pattern and range of services needed for problem drinkers said that there should be community-based services which acknowledged that different people required different types of help. This should lead to a flexible service which would aim at minimising the harm which problem drinkers caused for themselves and for others. It also stated that training and support for those working with alcohol-related problems was essential.

The present resources for coping with alcohol misuse have developed along these lines and, although there has been much progress, the service is still patchy and in one third of all Health Districts provision is poor or almost non-existent. The exact form in which support is given varies from place to place. In some Health Districts a comprehensive service will be provided directly by the Health Service, whilst in others it will be provided by the Alcohol Advisory Centre (AAC). Although the sources will vary, the services provided by a good set-up will be very similar. If the service is provided by the Mental Health Service it will be staffed largely by community psychiatric nurses, possibly with a social worker provided by the Social Services Department and with support from a consultant psychiatrist. The AAC is likely to be headed by a Director who is either a registered mental nurse or a social worker by training. The AACs often use volunteer counsellors, but they too are likely to be recruited from the appropriate professional backgrounds.

One important aspect of the provision is that it should be easily available with minimal waiting time. Many of these services are now accepting **self-referrals**. The AACs are often approached via the telephone directory. Their premises, which are usually central, normally operate a **drop-in facility**. This is much easier to provide in an urban setting and often the rural areas are less well served.

The pattern is now for the helping agency to provide a service both for problem drinkers and for their families and friends. They are likely to provide a counselling service, both individually and in support groups. Help is also given, where appropriate, by marital and family therapy sessions and by training in stress and anxiety management. Long-term follow-up can be provided. The AACs operate largely in their town centre offices or advisory centres whereas the Health Services community alcohol teams may undertake clinics in Health Centres or offer home visits by a psychiatric nurse.

Both the statutory and voluntary teams will provide an information service for the general public and a training facility for other professionals whose work involves them with problem drinkers. Many also provide services for specific groups such as women and ethnic minorities.

In 1989 the Office of Population Census Surveys stated that in this country there were $1\frac{1}{2}$ million people who were drinking at dangerous levels and a further $5\frac{1}{2}$ million whose drinking exceeded the accepted 'safe' levels. Government policy has moved towards the setting-up of an integrated service to combat the harm caused by alcohol misuse. The plans for **Care in the Community** stated that Health Authorities should develop plans for an alcohol service. Although the implementation of the plans for care in the community was delayed until 1993, in March 1990 the Government made a funding initiative of £3.8 million over three years to 'improve and extend the existing network of local Councils on Alcohol'. This funding is limited to voluntary organisations. Alcohol Concern have been given the task of allocating it appropriately. So far government funding for help with alcohol-related problems has taken the form of grant aid. However, during recent years there has been a shift in the type of funding relationships proposed, with the move towards the concept of contractual funding. It may well be that in future many of the country's services will be contracted out by the Health Service to the voluntary organisations.

T E N

Mental health and mental illness

10.1 Introduction

Mental health is defined in terms of behaviour and personality which fit in with the norms of the society in which one lives. If one is mentally healthy one can live successfully amongst one's fellows and function effectively both economically and socially. It follows that any definition of mental health will depend on the norms of the particular society. In some societies the concept of mental illness may not exist: people whom we would consider to be mentally ill may be revered as soothsayers, shamans and witch-doctors. Here, we consider those who have visual or auditory hallucinations, or who go into periods of withdrawal from society, or who become excessively elated, to be mentally ill, but elsewhere they are the seers into the future and determine the societal policies and actions. For the purposes of this book, mental illness will be considered in relation to Western society and the forms of mental illness recognised in Great Britain will be discussed.

Thus the general definition of **mental illness** to be used is that form of illness which presents mainly psychological symptoms and/or disturbances of behaviour which are incompatible with normal social functioning.

10.2 Historical review

Mental illness seems to have existed throughout the documentation of human history, with a fascinating progression in the ways in which it has been recorded. Biblical and other ancient documents contain many references to madness or mental illness, usually in terms of possession by devils or evil spirits. In fact this is a concept of mental illness which remained in common usage until quite modern times. The whole history of mental illness is clouded by fear and revulsion and throughout the centuries by a feeling that the mentally ill were evil. Another longstanding misapprehension about mental illness is that it is governed by the moon, hence the term **lunatic** which was in formal use during the nineteenth century and is still used in common parlance.

This fear, combined with, and indeed arising from, an ignorance of the

Figure 10.1 Bedlam, the eighteenth-century lunatic asylum, as portrayed in Hogarth's 'Rake's Progress'.

causes of mental illness together with a total lack of the concept of, or means of, treatment, led to appalling treatment of the mentally ill. Figure 10.1 gives an indication of the way in which those considered to be mentally ill were housed. In the eighteenth century they were locked up in gaols, poor-houses and bridewells in insanitary conditions, often being chained up, starved and beaten. It was by no means uncommon for people to visit the 'madhouses' to taunt and provoke the unfortunate inmates as a form of entertainment. At the same period a widespread phenomenon was private madhouses run for profit and it was quite common for people to be wrongfully detained in them. The law permitted the insane to be locked up in some secure place for as long as their madness was deemed to continue and for their property to be seized to pay for their maintenance.

At the beginning of the nineteenth century changes in the care of the mentally ill took place and, following legislation, the **County Asylums** were built. These were usually enormous, prison-like buildings constructed in remote rural areas, consequently they were a 'safe' distance away from centres of population. Many of these remain today, still used as psychiatric hospitals, albeit improved and upgraded to allow for modern standards and treatment methods. Also, as urbanisation has spread, they are now much nearer to or actually part of the towns which they serve.

In the middle of the nineteenth century, further legislation was passed which protected people against wrongful detention in asylums. The pattern of care of the mentally ill which developed was of **long-term custodial care**. People committed to the asylums usually remained there for life.

For almost a century the only way to gain admission to a mental hospital was by **certification** as insane and **compulsory detention**. It was not until 1930 that it became possible to choose to enter hospital as a voluntary patient, or equally important, to be able to make one's own decision to leave hospital. Until 1948 voluntary patients had to give 72 hours notice of their intention to leave hospital. Certification remained a judicial procedure rather than a medical one.

By the middle of the twentieth century the situation was changing again. Major developments were being made in the treatment of mental illness. Pharmacological research had produced a range of tranquilising drugs which replaced physical restraints such as **padded cells** or **strait-jackets** (heavy canvas suits into which patients were tied to restrain them). Drugs for the active treatment of mental illness such as **anti-depressants** and **neuroleptic** drugs (for the treatment of schizophrenia) became available. Other treatments were developed, particularly **electro-convulsive therapy** (ETC) which was very effective in treating deep depressions. The concept of mental illness changed from that of illness for which little could be offered other than life-long custodial care to illnesses many of which were characterised by relatively short acute episodes which, although they might recur, were amenable to treatment. From the 1970s onwards **psycho-therapy** also became more widely used as a valuable aid to recovery.

Along with these changes in treatment and recovery came changes in the law, particularly that relating to compulsory admission and treatment. The Mental Health Act 1959 removed the concept of certification of insanity, replacing it with that of **compulsory admission** to hospital for observation and treatment. The grounds for compulsory admission were that a person was mentally disordered, was unwilling to be admitted to or to stay in hospital and was a danger to him/herself or to others. The procedure for admission was taken from the courts and placed in the hands of doctors and social workers. It also placed considerable restriction on the length of time for which anyone could be detained in hospital.

A further Mental Health Act came into force in 1983. In essence this was similar to the 1959 Act but introduced further safeguards to the rights of the individual. It strengthened the good points of its predecessor and removed some inconsistencies. It shortened the length of time people could be detained without review, strengthened patients rights to appeal against detention, instituted independent reviews of some patients detained for the longer periods permissible and required independent medical 'second opinions' with regard to some treatments such as ECT. It also removed alcoholism as a sufficient medical reason for detention in hospital.

Although there are people who would argue that the mentally ill have the right to decide for themselves whether or not they are willing to enter hospital and accept treatment, on balance most people would acknowledge that on occasions mental illness is such that those who suffer from it do not have the insight to make reasonable decisions and it is in the interests of both the individual and society to ensure adequate and appropriate treatment for them. It seems likely that these provisions will remain in force for some time to come.

10.3 Changing pattern of psychiatric care

As we approach the end of the twentieth century the pattern of care of the mentally ill is changing radically. The Government are committed to the closure of the large mental hospitals and the provision of care in the community. The care of the acutely mentally ill will remain in hospitals but is being transferred to mental illness units or wards in local District General Hospitals. This has the advantages of providing care in local centres of population and of removing the stigma which still attaches to the old mental hospitals.

The other groups for which residential care has to be provided are the long-term chronically mentally ill and the elderly mentally frail (mainly dementias). The problem of **senile dementia** (see chapter 11) is one which is growing along with an ageing population. Many of these people will need permanent care and this is best provided in small units close to where they live. Moves are being made to extend or open such units in District General Hospitals or the more local, small, Community Hospitals.

The major challenge of the closure of the large mental hospitals is, however, to provide suitable care for the long-stay population, the bulk of whom suffer from **schizophrenia** (see chapter 12). Many of these people have been in hospital since their early twenties and expected to remain there forever. They have become **institutionalised**. In general, the aim is to provide a variety of accommodation to suit the level of dependency of its residents. This will vary from hostels with a fairly high level of staffing, through group homes where three or four people may share a house, to individual flats. They will be located in towns spread throughout the catchment area of the old hospitals.

One of the things to be considered in an undertaking of this kind is the cost. Good care in the community is not cheap. However, some of the old hospitals were very costly to run. The large old buildings had high maintenance costs. Many were spread over very large sites. It was not uncommon for wards within one hospital to be over a mile apart and the antiquated heating systems in these hospitals were wasteful of energy. In one large hospital it was found that 58% of its total budget went on maintaining the buildings alone. Again, many of these hospitals were built on large sites (often having included a hospital farm, which in the past had provided both food and occupation for the patients). This has now become prime building land and the government has stated that any monies raised by the sale of mental hospital buildings or land must be used for the development of care for the mentally ill.

Another difficulty encountered was that of preparing both patients and staff for such a radical change. This needs time and careful preparation. Patients (a high proportion of whom are single men) must be taught the skills of daily living including budgetting, shopping and cooking. The hospitals, whatever their faults, provide a social network for their patients' leisure and it is important that this must not be lost. Usually patients are prepared for discharge in small groups of friends who then move out into the community together. It is essential that a wide range of support services and facilities is available to mentally ill people living in the community. These will include **day hospitals** and **day centres**, **occupational** or **industrial therapy units** and **drop-in social centres**. Many psychiatric nurses who previously worked in hospital have become community psychiatric nurses and their regular visits to patients are crucial. There will also be a need for some of the units to have housekeepers who call in regularly to help with domestic chores and voluntary visitors who can help low-motivated people to cope with the stresses of independent life.

This all calls for a partnership between health authorities, local authorities (Social Services in particular, but also Housing Departments), Housing Associations and voluntary associations such as **MIND**.

Many areas are moving towards opening **Mental Health Centres** in centres of population. These, many of which are adjacent to Health Centres, act as a base for the various professionals, psychiatrists, nurses, occupational therapists and social workers and facilitate interdisciplinary communication. They can provide a base for out-patient clinics and therapy sessions and also provide a useful drop-in support and advice service for the community in general and for other caring professionals.

Transfer of long-term mentally ill people into the community will not be easy, particularly in the deprived inner city areas. Many people are, understandably, anxious about the setting-up of a hostel or home in their locality. The patients themselves are anxious about change and the greater demands which independent living will place upon them. There have been instances where large-scale discharges from hospital have caused problems, with numbers of under-occupied people housed in bed and breakfast accommodation. They have nothing to do to fill their time and spend their days aimlessly wandering the streets. This tends to happen if closures are rushed and underfunded.

To make such changes from institutional to community care successful takes time and careful preparation. In the Worcester area, which was one of the first to close its large psychiatric hospitals, a feasibility study was undertaken in 1970, the last new patients were admitted in 1978 and the hospital actually closed in 1989. This indicates the magnitude of, and the time scale for, such an undertaking.

The future promises well for the care of the mentally ill. The acutely ill will get their treatment within general hospitals which should reduce the stigma and fear of mental illness. The elderly mentally frail will be cared for in their own locality where they can be visited with relative ease by equally elderly friends and relations. With the passage of time, chronically ill patients who have not been institutionalised should settle well into small, local units and remain supported in the mainstream of life.

Alzheimer's disease and other dementias

11.1 Introduction

In the past **dementia** was a term used as a synonym for madness, but in modern usage it means a loss of or deterioration in intellectual abilities.

Dementia is an acquired brain disease which is both diffuse, affecting many parts of the brain, and chronic, that is long-term. The prevalence of all forms of dementia in the 65+ population is 5–7%. The age-related prevalence rises steeply to age 85–90, then levels off.

There are two main types of dementia in the elderly. These are **Alzheimer's disease** and **multi-infarct dementia**. In younger people, dementia is usually the result of an infection, traumatic event or the chronic misuse of alcohol or other drugs. Infections such as **encephalitis** or **meningitis** which cause damage to brain tissue may result in some degree of dementia. Dementia as a result of alcohol misuse may be acute or chronic, the signs and symptoms of each being very similar. The acute problem is **Wernicke's encephalopathy** and the chronic effect is **Korsakoff's psychosis**. In the former a confusional state and **ataxia** (uncoordination of voluntary muscle action, particularly in the muscle groups concerned with walking or reaching for objects) develop. The latter includes recent memory loss and often **confabulation** (inventing stories to fill memory gaps).

11.2 Alzheimer's disease

This condition was named after the psychiatrist who in 1907 first described this type of dementia occurring in middle-aged people (pre-senile dementia). Two types of Alzheimer's disease are recognised. These are **early onset** (middle age) and **late onset** (old age), though they may be the two ends of a continuum. However, there are noticeable differences between the two types. Late-onset Alzheimer's disease seems to be a largely cholinergic defect and there is no apparent genetic predisposition. The early-onset form shows widespread neurotransmitter change and a definite familial tendency or genetic predisposition. Alzheimer's disease occurs in members of all social groups in society and does not seem to be related to life stress events or to either an active or inactive life.

Neurological changes

There are many abnormal changes in the brain on a microscopical level. Degeneration of specific cells occurs, for example the cholinergic neurones in the basal forebrain. At post-mortem, two major changes are apparent. These are the presence of large numbers of **senile plaques** and **neurofibrillar tangles**. Senile plaques are found in the nerve cells of all ageing brains. These plaques have an **amyloid core**. Amyloid is a dense filamentous material composed of protein, at least part of which is immunoglobulin molecules. It has been suggested that the amyloid core represents antigen–antibody complexes which have been catabolised by phagocytes and degraded by lysosomes. Neurofibrillar tangles contain a protein similar to amyloid. These tangles are thickenings and contortions of fibrils in the neuronal cytoplasm. Another feature is that in the senile plaques there is always a high level of aluminium. The role of aluminium, if any, has not yet been ascertained. Aluminium accumulates in all ageing brains and so may not be tied specifically to the development of Alzheimer's disease.

Biochemical changes

There is much evidence to support the idea that changes in the cholinergic pathways in the brain are important in the pathology of Alzheimer's disease. As compared with controls, reductions to less than 25% of normal are seen in values for the activity of choline acetyl transferase and acetylcholine esterase. This reduction is seen in the frontal, parietal and hippocampal regions of the cerebral cortex. The loss is greatest in the **hippocampus**. The main problem seems to be a failure in the synthesis of acetylcholine, as reductions in this synthesis correlate with the degree of dementia present.

The exact mechanisms involved in this reduction in acetylcholine production are not known. At present, the reduced choline acetyl transferase activity is thought to be due to a failure in the uptake of choline either at the blood–brain barrier or at the nerve cell level. It was noted earlier that many cells in ageing brains contain a high level of aluminium. Aluminium can bind to **transferrin** which is a carrier of essential biological substances into brain tissue. This binding may well interfere with the normal passage of materials into the brain cells.

Causation of Alzheimer's disease

There are no certainties but many possibilities where causation is concerned. A genetic involvement in a number of cases has been noted. One certainty is that levels of amyloid protein are controlled by a gene on chromosome 21.

Individuals with Down's syndrome who have three chromosomes 21 have a very high risk of developing Alzheimer's disease if they live to middle age. This gene is switched on by factors which 'stress' the cells. Aluminium may be one of these factors.

Since Alzheimer's disease is age-related it is likely that failure of immune competence plays at least a part in its pathogenesis. This may be due to a progressive decline in the immune system's defence against toxins. Another possibility is the increased risk of failure to differentiate between 'self' and 'non-self' leading to the destruction of nerve cells. The increased activity of **T suppressor cells** in the elderly may also be important. The accumulation of aluminium may be an important factor but as this happens in all ageing brains it is probably not tied specifically to the development of Alzheimer's disease. Most researchers in the field subscribe to **'catch all' hypotheses** for causation. The consensus is that there is no one causative agent but many and various combinations of factors may all lead to the development of the disease.

Clinical features of Alzheimer's disease

Alzheimer-type dementia usually begins with memory impairment, particularly for recent events and information, followed by deterioration in speech, language and comprehension. The characteristic of this type of dementia is the steady decline of mental faculties and the disturbance of social behaviour. Deterioration in the activity of many parts of the cortex occurs, particularly that of the frontal, temporal and parietal lobes.

In the later stages there is the reappearance of **primitive reflexes** which have been suppressed since early childhood, for example the grasp, sucking and plantar extension reflexes. These occur when the frontal lobes fail to inhibit the subcortical motor areas. Temporal lobe involvement leads to the gradual loss of long-term as well as short-term memory, and the deterioration of the parietal lobes leads to the loss of ability to carry out fine or complex motor activities.

11.3 Multi-infarct dementia

Cerebral arteriosclerosis is very common in old age. Studies of the brains of demented and non-demented elderly people show no difference between the two groups in terms of either the degree or extent of arteriosclerosis. Thus, although both **cerebral haemorrhage** and **cerebral thrombosis** occur as a result of arteriosclerosis, these do not seem to be a major cause of dementia. When vascular disease is responsible for dementia in old age it is the result of multiple infarcts secondary to disease of the coronary and other extracranial arteries. This type of dementia is therefore called **multi-infarct dementia**.

An **infarct** is the death of a portion of the cardiac muscle. Each infarct gives rise to blood clots which, if they block a cerebral blood vessel may cause a stroke, large or small. Thus the history of this type of dementia is an **episodic** and **stepwise deterioration**, often with some degree of recovery after each **ischaemic episode** (a local diminution in the blood supply due to obstruction of the inflow of arterial blood). This type of dementia is often preceded by transient ischaemic episodes causing falls, short-lived confusion and difficulties with speech and language.

Cognitive impairment tends to be selective and uneven in multi-infarct dementia, unlike the pattern of widespread impairment in Alzheimer's disease. Common patterns are severe memory loss with well-preserved verbal ability or **dysphasia**, and memory loss with well-preserved insight, judgement and emotional control. Quite often the patients have suffered from moderate to severe depression before the onset of dementia.

In the region of 15–20% of dementias are vascular in origin and another 17% are of mixed origin.

11.4 Management and treatment of dementia

Whilst, as yet, we do not have any form of medication or other treatment which will stop the destruction of brain cells in dementia, there are ways in which the patient can be helped to function more effectively. One of the important things is to reduce **sensory deprivation** to a minimum. If we were placed in a darkened soundproof room we would quite quickly become somewhat disorientated in time and space. So if an old person with an unreliable memory has difficulty in seeing or hearing he or she can easily lose touch with reality. It is important that glasses and hearing aids are as effective as possible. It may be better to give up wearing bifocals which can be confusing, and return to single lenses with separate reading glasses.

Without a framework of time and space it is easy to become disorientated. This can be helped by a process known as **reality orientation** in which practical help is given to keep people in touch with reality. A reliable clock is very important, as is a calendar which is easy to read. A clock/calendar which automatically changes the date can be very helpful. **Memory cues** are also useful, examples are doors labelled and timetables for daily routines clearly written and prominently displayed. These things are now used widely in hospitals and old people's homes, but can also be used to advantage in people's own homes. If an old person is inclined to wander, it can be a help to have a clearly written notice pinned to the inside of the door reminding them not to go out until (say) their daughter calls in. Some people in the earlier stages of dementia may be helped by regular daily phone calls from family or friends to check that their normal daily routine is being maintained.

Knowing who you are is vital so it is important to call old people by their own names. Mirrors can be a useful aid to self-identification and self-esteem. It is also important to speak slowly and clearly in order that the elderly can hear and understand so that they do not feel isolated.

In dementia it is often recent memory which fails first, long-term memory remaining clearer and more intact. To maintain reality orientation it is important that one does not reinforce faulty memories. For example if old people talk about their childhood as if it were happening now, they should be gently reminded that it was a long time ago. However, it is possible to use this faculty of remembering long-gone events in a positive way. This is known as **reminiscence therapy** which includes, usually in a group situation, looking at old photographs, newspapers and objects and talking about them to help strengthen identity and self-esteem. Sometimes a confused, elderly person must feel unable to give the right answer to anything, and being able to talk clearly about youthful experiences may increase self-confidence. After talking together about the past, many memory-impaired old people are then able to orientate themselves and acknowledge that the things they have talked about were in the past, and relate them to the present.

Support for elderly people with dementia is much in demand, ranging from support in their own homes to long-term psychiatric care. These services include **Home Helps** and **Meals on Wheels**. Many **Day Centres** and **Day Hospitals for the elderly** are now setting aside one or two days a week when they take elderly confused people. Social Services provide residential care for the elderly in old people's homes and there is also a growing number of privately run Rest Homes for the elderly. Some of these homes look after mentally and physically frail old people together, whilst others may have a separate wing for the mentally frail. There are also homes which care exclusively for the dementing elderly.

Care of the more severe dementias is the province of the psychiatric services. They provide psychogeriatric assessment units. Sometimes these are sited along with the acute psychiatric services but sometimes they are located alongside geriatric assessment services. The long-term care of the dementias has traditionally been provided within the large psychiatric hospitals. However, as these close we are now moving towards the establishment of small, local units. These are often provided alongside general geriatric care in small Community Hospitals, in the form of separate psychogeriatric wards. They can provide a range of care, apart from permanent long-term care, depending on the needs of the individual families concerned. Other provisions include occasional respite or holiday care and programmed short-stay care. With programmed care, elderly demented people can remain at home for most of the time, but be admitted, usually for two-week periods, on a regular basis to give their families a break.

This support for carers is very important. However well a relative or friend appears to be coping, it is important that they should have good support. The statutory services can provide much of this support as discussed above, but there is an important role here for voluntary organisations such as **MIND** and **Age Concern**. They too can provide Day Centres and in many areas a valuable service in providing 'sitters-in' (a granny-sitting service rather like a baby-sitting service). In some places, carers have got together to form their own support group through local Alzheimer's Disease Societies or Carer's groups which can be extremely valuable.

Other mental illnesses

12.1 Schizophrenia

Although schizophrenia is a well-known mental illness and has been subject to much research, its causation is still uncertain. It is recognised only by its symptoms and the way in which it alters behaviour and functioning. The term **schizophrenia** means 'split mind'. This does not imply split into two distinct parts (Jekyll and Hyde) as is often believed by the layman, but that the mind is fragmented with disconnected thoughts and ideas.

The majority of sufferers develop the illness between the ages of 20 and 40 years. It tends to arise earlier in men than in women. Schizophrenia is a very variable illness which occurs in both acute and chronic forms. There is no single or even constant group of symptoms which are characteristic of the illness but many symptoms, both positive and negative, some of which will be present and which together give the diagnosis.

Positive symptoms
These are usually acute symptoms, often with a quite sudden onset. They include disturbances in the control of the patient's thoughts and various delusions and hallucinations. These often lead to restlessness and excitement. A common delusion in schizophrenia is that thoughts or actions are being controlled by an outside force. The hallucinations of schizophrenia are usually auditory ones. They can take the form of believing that one can hear one's thoughts spoken out loud, that one can hear voices talking about oneself (often in uncomplimentary terms) or that voices are commenting on what one is doing.

Negative symptoms
The important negative aspects of schizophrenia consist of impairment of the emotions and of drive or initiative. Emotional responsiveness decreases and may disappear totally leaving a person whose facial expression is wooden or mask-like and who lacks the normal, non-verbal means of communication by facial expression. This mood is usually decribed as **flat**.

It should be clear from the above that a combination of negative and positive symptoms can be very disabling indeed.

Schizophrenia is treated with **neuroleptic drugs**, the phenothiazines, which quickly control the restlessness and excitement. It is thought that these drugs act by blocking the dopamine receptors in the brain. Many schizophrenics need to take maintenance doses of these drugs indefinitely to remain controlled and symptom-free. Treatment by drugs has virtually no effect on the negative symptoms of the illness. These are best helped by a rehabilitation programme which may take a considerable time.

Most schizophrenics need long-term follow-up to ensure that their maintenance medication is continued and to support them both personally and socially. It is also very important that if a relapse occurs it should be treated very quickly to avoid the illness becoming firmly re-established.

Aetiology of schizophrenia

Schizophrenia tends to run in families and there is strong evidence that a predisposition to the illness is inherited. The expectancy rates for the development of schizophrenia rise with increasing relatedness to a sufferer. The incidence in the general population is only 1% but this rises to 50% or more for the co-twin of a monozygotic twin with schizophrenia. The various risks are shown in figure 12.1. Because the concordance in monozygotic twins is only 50%, plus the fact that children both of whose parents are schizophrenic have almost as high a risk, environmental factors also seem to have a large effect on the development of the illness.

Various genetic bases have been suggested, but two are the front runners. One of these is that there is a dominant gene with 25% penetration involved. This means that three-quarters of the carriers of the gene will not develop the illness. The second is that schizophrenia has polygenic inheritance with a few major genes and a number of modifying (supporter or suppressor) genes, which would mean that the genetic background varies from case to case. At present, this is the favoured hypothesis.

It seems likely that a genetic predisposition is necessary for the illness to develop, but whether or not it does so depends on environmental triggers or precipitating factors. Various biological hypotheses have been put forward to explain the development of schizophrenia but none has been upheld by ongoing research.

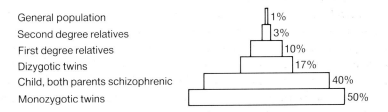

General population   1%
Second degree relatives   3%
First degree relatives   10%
Dizygotic twins   17%
Child, both parents schizophrenic   40%
Monozygotic twins   50%

Figure 12.1 Risk of schizophrenia in patient's relatives.

12.2 Affective disorders

These are illnesses in which the affect or mood is disturbed and in which the moods concerned range from **mania**, an extreme form of elation, to **depression**. Depression in varying degrees is a very common form of mental illness whilst mania (or **hypomania**, a less severe form) is much less common. These two illnesses are sometimes regarded as two separate illnesses and indeed there are many peope who suffer frequently from depression without ever becoming truly elated. Nowadays a more commonly held view is that depression and mania are the two extremes of a continuum of affect in which people swing to either side of the median point, some to a sufficient extent to suffer affective illness whilst the majority have mood changes which are considered to be within normal limits.

Within depression, two forms of the illness have been described. The more severe is known as **endogenous**, that is coming from within and having little or no relevance to the person's life situation. The milder form, known as **reactive depression**, is an illness which relates directly to life stress.

Genetic and biological factors in affective disorders

Genetic studies have consistently shown that there is a stronger inherited factor in manic depressive illness than there is in either mania or depression alone. Where **minor depressive illness** is concerned there is very little genetic involvement.

There has been difficulty in interpreting biochemical aspects of affective disorders because of the problem of separating cause and effect. The most acceptable biochemical hypothesis is that these illnesses are caused by anomalies with the monoamino neurotransmitters, mainly noradrenalin and serotonin.

Mania

Mania is much less common than depression. It is characterised by an elevation of mood, accelerated activity and often erratic behaviour. Although manic or hypomanic people can be **euphoric** (inappropriately cheerful) they can also become irritable and aggressive if family or friends try to restrain their unrealistic plans or actions. They are easily distractable, with rapid speech and grandiose ideas or delusions. This over-activity may lead to an inability to sleep and ultimately to total exhaustion.

Sufferers from mania show virtually no insight into their condition and often compulsory admission to mental hospital is necessary. Neither mania nor hypomania are amenable to psychotherapy. Both antipsychotic drugs and lithium carbonate are used in treatment, but the former are generally preferred as there are fewer dangers of toxic reactions. Fortunately, most episodes of mania are short-lived and respond well to treatment.

Depression

To be depressed is a concept which is familiar to all of us, so it must be stressed that there is a great difference between feeling low, fed-up and miserable which most people experience at some time and depression in its psychiatric sense.

Depressive illness affects both sexes but all forms of it are more common in women than in men. In the more severe forms of depression, mood is low, psychomotor activity diminishes and self-confidence vanishes to be replaced by feelings of guilt and worthlessness. The lowering of psychomotor activity includes a lack of facial expression, giving a mask-like face, and lowered vitality with virtually no spontaneous movements. Major depressive illness in which insight is lacking or limited is thought to have some biochemical basis and is usually treated initially by anti-depressant drugs.

In cases of very severe depression where the patient may become so retarded in activity that they are unable to speak, eat or drink or in cases which fail to respond to anti-depressant drugs, treatment by **electro-convulsive therapy** (ECT) is often successful. It is unfortunate that ECT has had very bad publicity in the past and has been feared by the general public. There are two reasons for this. One is that the whole concept of the 'electric shock' in lay language is couched in highly emotional terms and thus is quite frightening. The other is that in the early days (1950s) the treatment techniques were less well developed and, given without muscle relaxants or anaesthetics, the convulsions could cause fractures.

Minor depressive illness

Although this is a true form of depression, it presents quite differently from the more severe major depressive illness. Mood is depressed but the sufferer may become cheerful from time to time when in a favourable situation. In this illness there is no actual psychomotor retardation, but even so the sufferer may feel tired and lack energy. If sleep is disturbed there is usually a difficulty in getting to sleep rather than the problem of waking early in the morning. Often sufferers wake up in the morning feeling reasonably well, but as the day passes they remember the problems which depress them and feel worse at the end of the day, lying awake and worrying instead of falling asleep. In this form of depression, the link between precipitating events and the depression is more clearly seen and insight exists. This means that it can reasonably be called a neurotic illness and is often referred to as **reactive depression**. The precipitating event is often some form of loss such as the death of a loved one, the breakdown of a marriage or relationship, the loss of a job or the less specific 'loss of face'.

Mild depressive illness is best treated by psychotherapy; in a sensitive and supportive way the person is helped to bring the feelings of grief and worry into the open so that they can be accepted and he or she can come to terms with them. Sometimes social intervention can help by relieving some of the pressures which contributed to the depression. This may be help with budgetting where financial problems are overwhelming or help to change job or lifestyle to remove or at least minimise stress.

Manic depressive illness

Manic depressive illness may involve mood swings which occur in only part of the pendulum of affect (see figure 12.2). For example, they may suffer only from a depressive illness in which their mood will swing between normal and depressed. A few people however will suffer an illness in which they swing all the way between mania and depression.

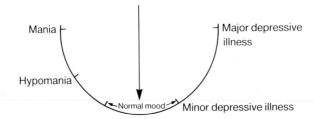

Figure 12.2 A pendulum diagram to illustrate the continuum concept of affective disorder.

12.3 Neurosis

The neurotic illnesses are the major group of psychiatric disorders from a numerical point of view, accounting for a high proportion of referrals to psychiatrists and certainly for the majority of psychiatric problems seen by general practitioners.

Although some neurotic disorders can have a severely disabling effect on a person, in general the neuroses are the least severe of the mental illnesses. Neurotic illness can be defined as an abnormal emotional reaction to life events, or an over-reaction to stress. The symptoms of neurosis, the most common being **anxiety**, are easily understood. In lay terms the neurotic person can be described as 'nervous' whereas the psychotic person is seen as 'mad'. Neurotic illnesses do not involve any organic disorder and insight into the illness is present, the personality remaining intact. We are all subject to stress and conflict, the differences between the normal and neurotic responses are defined by the degree and the appropriateness of those responses. Despite its misleading name, neurosis does not imply any malfunction of the nervous system.

Anxiety neurosis

Anxiety, when provoked by a potentially threatening situation, is a normal response. It is a biologically protective mechanism as it prepares the individual, both physically and psychologically, to cope with dangerous or difficult situations. This normal anxiety disappears when the stressful situation is dealt with by the normal alarm processes of the fight-or-flight reaction, regulated by the interaction of adrenalin and hormones antagonistic to it.

Neurotic anxiety states are those which arise as a response to a trivial or imagined threat and where the response is both greater than necessary and is unresolved. Severe anxiety states can cause distress and a long-term inability to function normally. They can sometimes be very resistant to treatment.

Phobias

Phobias are a form of anxiety neurosis but differ from general anxiety states in that they relate quite specifically to a particular stimulus. A **phobia** can be defined as an abnormal fear of an external object or situation which normally causes no concern to the majority of people.

The most common serious phobia is **agoraphobia** which derives its name from the Ancient Greek 'agora' meaning the market-place. Literally it means 'fear of the market place' and is a condition where the sufferers begin to develop symptoms of anxiety or panic when they leave home to go into a shopping centre or other crowded place.

Another more general, diffuse form of phobia is that of **social phobia** in which there is a fear of social situations, particularly formal ones. There is often a fear of eating in public which arises from a fear of doing something inept or foolish or from a feeling of insecurity. It usually occurs in early adult life and often resolves itself as the person gets older.

The most effective treatment available for phobic states is that of **behaviour therapy**. This approach is based on learning theory and is a clinical application of techniques developed in experimental psychology. Treatment aims at removing symptoms which are seen as maladaptive responses by learning new and better responses.

Obsessive compulsive disorders

Obsessional disorders are those in which a person has a compulsion to carry out a particular act, often repetitively, or to dwell on certain thoughts, at the same time realising that these actions or thoughts are pointless and ridiculous. It is not a common illness.

Obsessional neurosis has its counterpart in normal behaviour, particularly in childhood, often featuring in children's games. This is seen in the need to avoid stepping on cracks in the pavement or having to touch every third lamp-post, and so on. Similar behaviours are seen in the ceremonial rituals of some primitive societies. This type of behaviour in children usually disappears with maturity, but many perfectly normal adults show occasional obsessive symptoms such as the unnecessary checking that lights have been switched off or doors locked. Although many people experience mildly obsessive thoughts at times, this is not regarded as pathological. However, when obsessive thoughts or actions lead to interference with normal function they can constitute a most disabling and intractable illness.

12.4 Anorexia nervosa

Anorexia is an illness which largely affects adolescent girls, usually just after the onset of puberty. It is estimated that 1 in 150 adolescent girls are affected, which is about 15 times the frequency for adolescent boys. The illness is characterised by a severe loss in weight due to a refusal to eat, in girls by amenorrhoea (lack of menstrual periods), and by a specific psychological state in which there is an abnormal fear of fatness and a desire to be thin. Equivalent symptoms occur in male anorexics.

There are several factors which contribute to the development of anorexia nervosa. Whilst they are not in themselves a primary cause, it is probable that sociocultural factors play a part. Anorexia nervosa is an illness which is more frequent in social classes I, II and III than it is in IV and V. The tendency in the Western world to idealise and admire slimness and a consequent preoccupation with dieting may be a significant trigger factor in girls who are predisposed. Indeed, certain groups where a thin body image is important, such as ballet or theatrical schools, show an above-average incidence of anorexia nervosa. It is still relatively rare in Afro-Asian populations.

The anorexic girl is likely to grossly over-estimate the size of her own body and so insist that she is repulsively overweight when in reality her weight has dropped to a dangerous level. This fantasy situation is represented in figure 12.3.

Girls suffering from anorexia nervosa often experience a strong feeling of inadequacy and ineffectiveness. They attempt to achieve control in their lives but only achieve this in the area of eating, or rather refusing to eat. These girls are often immature psychologically and unable to cope with the challenges of puberty and their emerging sexuality. The cessation of

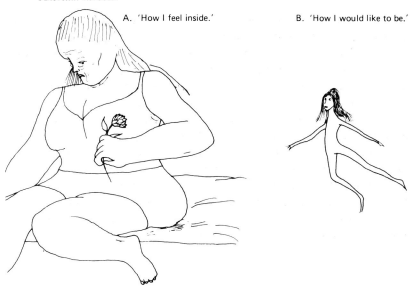

A. 'How I feel inside.'   B. 'How I would like to be.'

Figure 12.3 An anorexic girl's representation of her feelings about her body, drawn when she weighed 40 kg.

menstruation and the loss of feminine curves can enable the girl to retreat into a child-like state in which she feels safe.

The family dynamics in the families of anorexic girls are often precarious. Many of these families contain rigid or inadequate personalities who manage to develop a family structure in which they can function but who are ill-equipped to cope with change or challenge. They may present as a united family within which nobody rebels or argues, this being the only way in which they can survive.

The illness usually starts between 14 and 18 with dieting causing a rapid severe weight loss which soon goes beyond all reasonable limits. This weight loss can be as much as 20 kg in 3–6 months. The dieting may be reinforced by the use of purgatives or laxatives. Amenorrhoea often occurs quite early in the stage of rapid weight loss.

Psychologically the anorexic is preoccupied with her thinness and will often set herself a maximum weight above which she will not go. This will be much below her optimum weight. Paradoxically, she may show a great interest in food and insist on cooking lavish meals for her family. With the loss of weight and malnutrition, severe personality changes may occur. Social life may contract and the girl may stay reclusively at home. Sexual contact is avoided. Relationships within the family deteriorate as attempts to bully or bribe her into eating fail, and she may react in an aggressive way.

Anorexia nervosa is an illness from which recovery is slow. It often takes from 2–4 years and in some cases longer. Occurring as it does in adolescence and early adulthood, it can have a considerable adverse effect on academic and career prospects.

Bulimia nervosa is a variant of anorexia nervosa which sometimes occurs in the chronic phase of the illness in slightly older girls. It is characterised by irresistible urges to over-eat on forbidden, fattening foods such as fried food or cream cakes. These binges are followed immediately by self-induced vomiting and the abuse of purgatives. Bulimics usually have a body weight nearer to normal and may also menstruate. The frequent vomiting and purging may cause physical effects including serum electrolyte imbalance and frequent recurrent infections.

Treatment of anorexia nervosa is likely to be prolonged. The initial treatment is to overcome the effects of weight loss and malnutrition. This is essentially life-saving as untreated anorexics can die of starvation. It is important to gain the cooperation of the anorexic, not an easy task as many deny their illness. It is almost always necessary to undertake this phase of treatment in hospital under a caring but strict regime.

This phase of weight gain is usually supported by a form of behaviour therapy known as **operant conditioning** based on rewarding achievement. Initially the girl is cared for in a closely supervised and somewhat restrictive way, remaining in bed, not having visitors and so on. As target weights are achieved restrictions are eased and privileges earned, that is getting out of bed, receiving letters and visitors, going home for weekends and finally discharge from hospital.

After weight gain and a general improvement in physical health anorexics often become more outgoing and are able to talk about their problems. Regular supportive psychotherapy then becomes relevant and important. This will be needed on a long-term basis, for a year or more to prevent relapse. Consistent support from family and friends is also very important to maintain recovery.

Of girls who were severely ill, only about 40% recover fully whilst the recovery rate for mild cases is about 80% (no figures are available for boys as so few are affected). The others still show low body weight and irregular menstruation five years or more after the onset of the illness. A small percentage have periodic episodes of anorexia for many years after the initial illness.

Further reading

Drugs

Ashton M. (ed.) (1990) *Drug misuse in Britain 1990*, ISDD.
DHSS (1988) *Aids and drug misuse*, HMSO.
Edwards G. & Lader M. (eds.) (1990) *The nature of drug dependence*, Oxford.
Ghodse H. (1989) *Drugs and addictive behaviour*, Blackwell.
Pearson G., Gilman M. & Mc Iver S. (1987) *Young people and heroin*, Gower.
Ray O. & Ksir C. (1987) *Drugs, society and human behaviour* (4th ed.), Times Mirror/Mosby St Louis.
Robertson R. (1987) *Heroin, aids and society*, Hodder & Stoughton.

Alcohol

Alcohol Concern (1991) *Warning: Alcohol can damage your health*, Alcohol Concern.
British Medical Association (1988) *The drinking driver*, BMA.
Goddard E. (1991) *Drinking in England and Wales in the late 1980s*, OPCS.
McColville B. (1991) *Women under the influence: alcohol and its impact*, Grafton.
Plant M. (1985) *Women, drinking and pregnancy*, Tavistock.
Royal College of Physicians (1987) *A great and growing evil*, Tavistock.

Mental health

Burningham S. (1989) *Not on your own, the MIND guide to mental health*, Penguin.
Fraser M. (1987) *Dementia, its nature and management*, Wiley.
Freeman H.L. (1984) *Mental health and the environment*, Churchill Livingstone.

Index